HANDBOOK OF GLASS SCIENCE

HANDBOOK OF GLASS SCIENCE

By
Dr. Ajit Kumar Sharma
Deptt. of Physics
D.A.V. (P.G.) College
Bulandshahr (U.P.)
(India)

D P H

DISCOVERY PUBLISHING HOUSE PVT. LTD.
NEW DELHI-110 002

Published by:
Tilak Wasan
DISCOVERY PUBLISHING HOUSE PVT. LTD.
4383/4A, Ansari Road, Darya Ganj
New Delhi-110 002 (India)
Phone : +91-11-23279245, 43596064-65
Fax : +91-11-23253475
E-mail : parul.wasan@gmail.com
discoverypublishinghouse@gmail.com
web : www.discoverypublishinggroup.com

***First Edition:* 2012**
ISBN: 978-93-5056-094-5

Handbook of Glass Science

Printed at:
Shree Balaji Art Press
Delhi

Preface

A glass is an amorphous (non-crystalline) solid material. Glasses are typically brittle, and often optically transparent. Glass is commonly used for windows, bottles, modern hard drives and eyewear, and examples of glassy materials include soda-lime glass, borosilicate glass, acrylic glass, sugar glass, Muscovy-glass, and aluminium oxynitride. The term *glass* developed in the late Roman Empire. It was in the Roman glassmaking centre at Trier, now in modern Germany, that the late-Latin term *glesum* originated, probably from a Germanic word for a transparent, lustrous substance.

Strictly speaking, a glass is defined as an inorganic product of fusion which has been cooled through its glass transition to the solid state without crystallising. Many glasses contain silica as their main component and *glass former*. The term 'glass' is, however, often extended to all amorphous solids (and melts that easily form amorphous solids), including plastics, resins, or other silica-free amorphous solids. In addition, besides traditional melting techniques, any other means of preparation are considered, such as ion implantation, and the sol-gel method. Commonly, *glass science* and physics deal only with inorganic amorphous solids, while plastics and similar organics are covered by polymer science, biology and further scientific disciplines.

Glass plays an essential role in science and industry. The optical and physical properties of glass make it suitable for applications such as flat glass, container glass, optics and optoelectronics material, laboratory equipment, thermal insulator (glass wool), reinforcement fibre (glass-reinforced plastic, glass fibre reinforced concrete), and art.

The standard definition of a glass (or vitreous solid) is a solid formed by rapid melt quenching. If the cooling is sufficiently rapid (relative to the characteristic crystallization time) then crystallization is prevented and instead the disordered atomic configuration of the supercooled liquid is frozen into the solid state at the glass transition temperature T_g. Generally, the structure of a glass exists in a metastable state with respect to its crystalline form, although in certain circumstances, for example in atactic polymers, there is no crystalline analogue of the amorphous phase. As in other amorphous solids, the atomic structure of a glass lacks any long range translational periodicity. However, due to chemical bonding characteristics glasses do possess a high degree of short-range order with respect to local atomic polyhedra. It is deemed that the bonding structure of glasses, although disordered, has the same symmetry signature (Hausdorff-Besicovitch dimensionality) as for crystalline materials.

In order to make glass from materials with poor glass forming tendencies, novel techniques are used to increase cooling rate, or reduce crystal nucleation triggers.

Naturally occurring glass, especially obsidian, has been used by many Stone Age societies across the globe for the production of sharp cutting tools and, due to its limited source areas, was extensively traded. But in general, archaeological evidence suggests that the first true glass was made in coastal north Syria, Mesopotamia or Old Kingdom Egypt. Due to Egypt's favourable environment for preservation, the majority of well-studied early glass is found in Egypt, although some of this is likely to have been imported. The earliest known glass objects, of the mid third millennium BC, were beads, perhaps initially created as accidental by-products of metal-working slags or during the production of faience, a pre-glass vitreous material made by a process similar to glazing.

Author

Contents

Preface

1. **Introduction** 1
Glass Ingredients; Contemporary Glass Production; Silica-free Glasses; Physics of Glass; Glass *Vs.* a Supercooled Liquid; Behaviour of Antique Glass; Optical Waveguides; India (Hindu Kingdoms); Murano Glassmaking; Museums

2. **Physics of Glass** 18
Domains and Defects; Dislocations and Melting; Viscoelasticity; Early Work; Elastic Waves; Heat Transport; Electronic Structure

3. **Glass Transition** 33
Phosphates; Chalcogenides; Amorphous Metals; Biomaterials; Glass-ceramics; Colloidal Glasses

4. **Porous Glass** 45
Definition; Applications

5. **Sol-Gel** 50
Uniformity; Particles and Polymers; Polymerization; Applications

6. **Glass Production** 59
Glass Container Factories; Furnace; Forming Process; Internal Treatment; Annealing; Inspection Equipment; Secondary Processing; Packaging; Cold End; Coatings; Ancillary Processes — Compressors and Cooling; Marketing;

Lifecycle Impact; Local Environmental Impacts; Global Environmental Impact; Float Glass; Manufacture; Borosilicate Glass; Manufacturing Process; Composition and Physical Characteristics; Borosilicate Nanoparticles; In Lampworking

7. **Optical Lens Design** 75
Design Requirements; Process; Lens Optimization

8. **Glass Colouring** 80
Dichroic Glass

9. **History of Optics** 83
Early History of Optics; The Beginnings of Geometrical Optics; The Beginnings of Physical Optics; The Beginnings of Physiological Optics; Optics in Mediaeval Europe; Renaissance and Early Modern Optics; The Beginnings of Diffractive Optics; Lenses and Lensmaking; Quantum Optics

10. **Stained Glass** 100
Glass Production— Cylinder Glass— Crown Glass— Table Glass— Flashed Glass— Modern Production of Traditional Glass; Creating Stained Glass Windows; Origins; The Renaissance and Reformation; Revival in Britain; Revival in France; Revival in Europe; Twentieth Century

11. **Glass in Islamic Culture** 111
Technological Change; Middle Islamic Glass: Late 12th to Late 14th Century A.D.; Late Islamic Glass: 15th to Mid 19th Century A.D.; The Roles of Islamic Glass; Study of Islamic Glass

12. **Mirror** 120
Manufacturing; Effects; Safety and Easier Viewing; Televisions and Projectors; Instruments; Face-to-face Mirrors; Seasonal Lighting; Decoration; Entertainment; Art; Literature; Mirrors and Superstition

13. **Studio Glass** 136

Italy; United Kingdom; China; Japan; Australia; Mexico; The Netherlands; Belgium; Creating Art Made from Glass

14. **Glassblowing** 144

Free-blowing; In Modern Context; Origins; Recent Developments

15. **Glass Beadmaking** 152

Wound Glass Beads; Drawn Glass Beads; Molded Beads; Dichroic Glass Beads; Furnace Glass; Lead Crystal; Other Methods for Making Glass Beads

16. **Roman Glass** 157

Glass Working; Cold-cut Vessels

17. **Glass-reinforced Plastic** 168

Sizing; Applications; Storage Tanks; House Building; Fiberglass Spray Lay-up Operation; Chopped Strand Mat

18. **Amorphous Solid** 174

19. **Lens (Optics)** 178

Construction of Simple Lenses

20. **Transparency and Translucency** 183

Light Scattering; Multi-phonon Absorption; Light Scattering in Ceramics; Applications

21. **Fibreglass** 198

Chemistry; Properties; Safety; Glass-reinforced Plastic; Role of Recycling in Fibreglass Manufacturing

22. **Composite Material** 205

History; Moulding Methods; Vacuum Bag Moulding; Pressure Bag Moulding; Autoclave Moulding; Resin Transfer Moulding (RTM);

Tooling; Mechanics; Resins; Categories of Fibre-reinforced Composite Materials; Failure; Materials; Products

23. **Strength of Glass** **217**

Strength Types; Griffith Defects; Weibull Statistics; Intrinsic Strength; Pristine Fibres; Extrinsic Strength; Inert Strength; Theoretical Strength

Index *227*

1

Introduction

A *glass* is an amorphous (non-crystalline) solid material. Glasses are typically brittle, and often optically transparent. Glass is commonly used for windows, bottles, modern hard drives and eyewear, and examples of glassy materials include soda-lime glass, borosilicate glass, acrylic glass, sugar glass, Muscovy-glass, and aluminium oxynitride. The term *glass* developed in the late Roman Empire. It was in the Roman glassmaking centre at Trier, now in modern Germany, that the late-Latin term *glesum* originated, probably from a Germanic word for a transparent, lustrous substance.

Strictly speaking, a glass is defined as an inorganic product of fusion which has been cooled through its glass transition to the solid state without crystallising. Many glasses contain silica as their main component and *glass former.* The term 'glass' is, however, often extended to all amorphous solids (and melts that easily form amorphous solids), including plastics, resins, or other silica-free amorphous solids. In addition, besides traditional melting techniques, any other means of preparation are considered, such as ion implantation, and the sol-gel method. Commonly, *glass science* and physics deal only with inorganic amorphous solids, while plastics and similar organics are covered by polymer science, biology and further scientific disciplines.

Glass plays an essential role in science and industry. The optical and physical properties of glass make it suitable for applications such as flat glass, container glass, optics and optoelectronics material, laboratory equipment, thermal insulator (glass wool), reinforcement fibre (glass-reinforced plastic, glass fibre reinforced concrete), and art.

Glass Ingredients

Pure silica (SiO_2) has a 'glass melting point'— at a viscosity of 10 Pa·s (100 P) — of over 2300°C (4200°F). While pure silica can be made into glass for special applications (see fused quartz), other substances are added to common glass to simplify processing. One is sodium carbonate (Na_2CO_3), which lowers the melting point to about 1500°C (2700°F) in soda-lime glass; 'soda' refers to the original source of sodium carbonate in the soda ash obtained from certain plants. However, the soda makes the glass water soluble, which is usually undesirable, so lime (calcium oxide (CaO), generally obtained from limestone), some magnesium oxide (MgO) and aluminium oxide (Al_2O_3) are added to provide for a better chemical durability. The resulting glass contains about 70 to 74 per cent silica by weight and is called a soda-lime glass. Soda-lime glasses account for about 90 per cent of manufactured glass.

As well as soda and lime, most common glass has other ingredients added to change its properties. Lead glass, such as lead crystal or flint glass, is more 'brilliant' because the increased refractive index causes noticeably more 'sparkles', while boron may be added to change the thermal and electrical properties, as in Pyrex. Adding barium also increases the refractive index. Thorium oxide gives glass a high refractive index and low dispersion, and was formerly used in producing high-quality lenses, but due to its radioactivity has been replaced by lanthanum oxide in modern eye glasses. Large amounts of iron are used in glass that absorbs infrared energy, such as heat absorbing filters for movie projectors, while cerium(IV) oxide can be used for glass that absorbs UV wavelengths (biologically damaging ionizing radiation).

Another common glass ingredient is 'cullet' (recycled glass). The recycled glass saves on raw materials and energy. However, impurities in the cullet can lead to product and equipment failure.

Finally, fining agents such as sodium sulfate, sodium chloride, or antimony oxide are added to reduce the bubble content in the glass. Glass batch calculation is the method by which the correct raw material mixture is determined to achieve the desired glass composition.

Contemporary Glass Production

Following the glass batch preparation and mixing, the raw materials are transported to the furnace. Soda-lime glass for mass production is melted in gas fired units. Smaller scale furnaces for specialty glasses include electric melters, pot furnaces, and day tanks.

After melting, homogenization and refining (removal of bubbles), the glass is formed. Flat glass for windows and similar applications is formed by the float glass process, developed between 1953 and 1957 by Sir Alastair Pilkington and Kenneth Bickerstaff of the UK's Pilkington Brothers, who created a continuous ribbon of glass using a molten tin bath on which the molten glass flows unhindered under the influence of gravity. The top surface of the glass is subjected to nitrogen under pressure to obtain a polished finish. Container glass for common bottles and jars is formed by blowing and pressing methods. Further glass forming techniques are summarized in the table Glass forming techniques.

Once the desired form is obtained, glass is usually annealed for the removal of stresses. Surface treatments, coatings or lamination may follow to improve the chemical durability (glass container coatings, glass container internal treatment), strength (toughened glass, bulletproof glass, windshields), or optical properties (insulated glazing, anti-reflective coating).

New chemical glass compositions or new treatment techniques can be initially investigated in small-scale laboratory experiments. The raw materials for laboratory-scale glass melts are often different from those used in mass production because the cost factor has a low priority. In the laboratory mostly pure chemicals are used. Care must be taken that the raw materials have not reacted with moisture or other chemicals in the environment (such as alkali oxides and hydroxides, alkaline earth oxides and hydroxides, or boron oxide), or that the impurities are quantified (loss on ignition). Evaporation losses during glass melting should be considered during the selection of the raw materials, e.g., sodium selenite may be preferred over easily evaporating SeO_2. Also, more readily reacting raw materials may be preferred over relatively inert ones, such as $Al(OH)_3$ over Al_2O_3. Usually, the melts are carried out in platinum crucibles to reduce contamination from the crucible material. Glass homogeneity is achieved by homogenizing the raw materials mixture (glass batch), by stirring the melt, and by crushing and re-melting the first melt. The obtained glass is usually annealed to prevent breakage during processing.

In order to make glass from materials with poor glass forming tendencies, novel techniques are used to increase cooling rate, or reduce crystal nucleation triggers. Examples of these techniques include aerodynamic levitation (the melt is cooled whilst floating in a gas stream), splat quenching, (the melt is pressed between two metal anvils) and roller quenching (the melt is poured through rollers).

Silica-free Glasses

Besides common silica-based glasses, many other inorganic and organic materials may also form glasses, including plastics (e.g., acrylic glass), carbon, metals, carbon dioxide (*see below*), phosphates, borates, chalcogenides, fluorides, germanates (glasses based on GeO_2), tellurites (glasses based on TeO_2), antimonates (glasses based on Sb_2O_3), arsenates (glasses based on As_2O_3), titanates (glasses based on TiO_2), tantalates (glasses based on Ta_2O_5), nitrates, carbonates and many other substances.

Some glasses that do not include silica as a major constituent may have physico-chemical properties useful for their application in fibre optics and other specialized technical applications. These include fluoride glasses (fluorozirconates, fluoroaluminates), aluminosilicates, phosphate glasses and chalcogenide glasses.

Under extremes of pressure and temperature solids may exhibit large structural and physical changes which can lead to polyamorphic phase transitions. In 2006 Italian scientists created an amorphous phase of carbon dioxide using extreme pressure. The substance was named amorphous carbonia(a-CO_2) and exhibits an atomic structure resembling that of Silica.

Physics of Glass

Unsolved problems in physics: *What is the nature of the transition between a fluid or regular solid and a glassy phase? What are the physical mechanisms giving rise to the general properties of glasses?*

The amorphous structure of glassy Silica (SiO_2) in two dimensions. No long range order is present, however there is local ordering with respect to the tetrahedral arrangement of Oxygen (O) atoms around the Silicon (Si) atoms.

The standard definition of a glass (or vitreous solid) is a solid formed by rapid melt quenching. If the cooling is sufficiently rapid (relative to the characteristic crystallization time) then crystallization is prevented and instead the disordered atomic configuration of the supercooled liquid is frozen into the solid state at the glass transition temperature T_g. Generally, the structure of a glass exists in a metastable state with respect to its crystalline form, although in certain circumstances, for example in atactic polymers, there is no crystalline analogue of the amorphous phase. As in other amorphous solids, the atomic structure of a glass lacks any long range translational periodicity. However, due to chemical bonding characteristics glasses do possess a high degree of short-range order with respect to local atomic polyhedra. It is deemed that the bonding structure of glasses, although disordered, has the same symmetry signature (Hausdorff-Besicovitch dimensionality) as for crystalline materials.

Glass *vs.* a Supercooled Liquid

Glass is generally classed as an amorphous solid rather than a liquid. Glass displays all the mechanical properties of a solid. The notion that glass flows to an appreciable extent over extended periods of time is not supported by empirical research or theoretical analysis. From a more commonsense point of view, glass should be considered a solid since it is rigid according to everyday experience.

Some people consider glass to be a liquid due to its lack of a first-order phase transition where certain thermodynamic variables such as volume, entropy and enthalpy are discontinuous through the glass transition range. However, the glass transition may be described as analogous to a second-order phase transition where the intensive thermodynamic variables such as the thermal expansivity and heat capacity are discontinuous. Despite this, the equilibrium theory of phase transformations in solids does not entirely hold for glass, and hence the glass transition cannot be classed as one of the classical equilibrium phase transformations in solids.

Although the atomic structure of glass shares characteristics of the structure in a supercooled liquid, glass tends to behave as a solid below its glass transition temperature. A supercooled liquid behaves as a liquid, but it is below the freezing point of the material, and will crystallize almost instantly if a crystal is added as a core. The change in heat capacity at a glass transition and a melting transition of comparable materials are typically of the same order of magnitude, indicating that the change in active degrees of freedom is comparable as well. Both in a glass and in a crystal it is mostly only the vibrational degrees of freedom that remain active, whereas rotational and translational motion is arrested. This helps to explain why both crystalline and non-crystalline solids exhibit rigidity on most experimental time scales.

Behaviour of Antique Glass

The observation that old windows are often thicker at the bottom than at the top is often offered as supporting evidence for the view that glass flows over a matter of centuries. It is then assumed that the glass was once uniform, but has flowed to its new shape, which is a property of liquid. In actuality, the reason for this is that when panes of glass were commonly made by glassblowers, the technique used was to spin molten glass so as to create a round, mostly flat and even plate. This plate was then cut to fit a window. The pieces were not, however, absolutely flat; the edges of the disk became thicker as the glass spun. When actually installed in a window frame, the glass would be placed thicker side down both for the sake of stability and to prevent water accumulating in the lead cames at the bottom of the window. Occasionally such glass has been found thinner side down or thicker on either side of the window's edge, as would be caused by carelessness at the time of installation.

Mass production of glass window panes in the early twentieth century caused a similar effect. In glass factories, molten glass was poured onto a large cooling table and allowed to spread. The resulting glass is thicker at the location of the pour, located at the centre of the large sheet. These sheets were cut into smaller window panes with non-uniform thickness. Modern glass intended for windows is produced as float glass and is very uniform in thickness.

Several other points exemplify the misconception of the 'cathedral glass' theory:

> Writing in the American Journal of Physics, physicist Edgar D. Zanotto states "... the predicted relaxation time for GeO_2 at room temperature is 10^{32} years. Hence, the relaxation period (characteristic flow time) of cathedral glasses would be even longer." (10^{32} years is many times longer than the estimated age of the Universe.)

If mediaeval glass has flowed perceptibly, then ancient Roman and Egyptian objects should have flowed proportionately more — but this is not observed. Similarly, prehistoric obsidian blades should have lost their edge; this is not observed either (although obsidian may have a different viscosity from window glass).

If glass flows at a rate that allows changes to be seen with the naked eye after centuries, then the effect should be noticeable in antique telescopes. Any slight deformation in the antique telescopic lenses would lead to a dramatic decrease in optical performance, a phenomenon that is not observed.

There are many examples of centuries-old glass shelving which has not bent, even though it is under much higher stress from gravitational loads than vertical window glass.

Some glasses have a glass transition temperature close to or below room temperature. The behaviour of a material that has a glass transition close to room temperature depends upon the timescale during which the material is manipulated. If the material is hit it may break like a solid glass, but if the material is left on a table for a week it may flow like a liquid. This simply means that for the fast timescale its transition temperature is above room temperature, but for the slow one it is below. The shift in temperature with timescale is not very large however, as indicated by the transition of polypropylene glycol of -72°C and -71°C over different timescales. To observe window glass flowing as liquid at room temperature we would have to wait a much longer time than any human can exist. Therefore it is safe to consider a glass a solid far enough below its transition temperature: Cathedral glass does not flow because its glass transition temperature is many hundreds of degrees above room temperature. Close to this temperature there are interesting time-dependent properties. One of these is known as aging. Many polymers that we use in daily life such as polystyrene and polypropylene are in a glassy state but they are not too far below their glass transition temperature as opposed to rubber which is used above its glass transition temperature. Their mechanical properties may well change over time and this is serious concern when applying these materials in construction. In general for polymers there is a relation between the glass transition temperature and the speed of the deformation.

Many glasses have a chemical composition which includes what are referred to as absorption centres. This may cause them to be selective in their absorption of visible lightwaves (or white light frequencies). They absorb certain portions of the visible spectrum, while reflecting others. The frequencies of the spectrum which are not absorbed are either reflected back or transmitted for our physical observation. This is what gives rise to colour.

Thus, colour in glass may be obtained by addition of electrically charged ions (or colour centres) that are homogeneously distributed, and by precipitation of finely dispersed particles (such as in photochromic glasses). Ordinary soda-lime glass appears colourless to the naked eye when it is thin, although iron(II) oxide (FeO) impurities of up to 0.1 wt per cent produce a green tint which can be viewed in thick pieces or with the aid of scientific instruments. Further FeO and Cr_2O_3 additions may be used for the production of green bottles. Sulfur, together with carbon and iron salts, is used to form iron polysulfides and produce amber glass ranging from yellowish to almost black. Manganese dioxide can be added in small amounts to remove the green tint given by iron(II) oxide.

Optical Waveguides

Optically transparent materials focus on the response of a material to incoming light waves of a range of wavelengths. Frequency selective optical filters can be utilized to alter or enhance the brightness and contrast of a digital image. Guided light wave transmission via frequency selective waveguides involves the emerging field of fibre optics and the ability of certain glassy compositions as a transmission medium for a range of frequencies simultaneously (multimode optical fibre) with little or no interference between competing wavelengths or frequencies. This resonant mode of energy and data transmission via electromagnetic (light) wave propagation, though low powered, is relatively lossless.

An optical fibre is a cylindrical dielectric waveguide that transmits light along its axis by the process of total internal reflection. The fibre consists of a core surrounded by a cladding layer. To confine the optical signal in the core, the refractive index of the core must be greater than that of the cladding. The index of refraction is a way of measuring the speed of light in a material. (*Note:* The index of refraction is the ratio of the speed of light in a vacuum to the speed of light in a given medium. (The index of refraction of a vacuum is therefore equal to 1, by definition). The larger the index of refraction, the more slowly light travels in that medium. Typical values for core and cladding of an optical fibre are 1.48 and 1.46, respectively.

When light travelling in a dense medium hits a boundary at a steep angle, the light will be completely reflected. This effect is used in optical fibres to confine light in the core. Light travels along the fibre bouncing back and forth off of the boundary. Because the light must strike the boundary with an angle greater than the critical angle, only light that enters the fibre within a certain range of angles will be propagated. This range of angles is called the acceptance cone of the fibre. The size of this acceptance cone is a function of the refractive index difference between the fibre's core and cladding.

Optical waveguides are used as components in integrated optical circuits (e.g. light-emitting diodes, LEDs) or as the transmission medium in local and long haul optical communication systems. Also of value to materials science is the sensitivity of materials to thermal radiation in the infrared (IR) portion of the EM spectrum. This infrared homing (or 'heat-seeking') capability is responsible for such diverse optical phenomena as 'night vision' and IR luminescence.

Naturally occurring glass, especially obsidian, has been used by many Stone Age societies across the globe for the production of sharp cutting tools and, due to its limited source areas, was extensively traded. But in general, archaeological evidence suggests that the first true glass was made in coastal north Syria, Mesopotamia or Old Kingdom Egypt. Due to Egypt's favourable environment for preservation, the majority of well-studied early glass is found in Egypt, although some of this is likely to have been imported. The earliest known glass objects, of the mid third millennium BC, were beads, perhaps initially created as accidental by-products of metal-working slags or during the production of faience, a pre-glass vitreous material made by a process similar to glazing.

During the Late Bronze Age in Egypt and Western Asia there was a rapid growth in glass-making technology.

Archaeological finds from this period include coloured glass ingots, vessels (often coloured and shaped in imitation of highly prized hardstone carvings in semi-precious stones) and the ubiquitous beads. The alkali of Syrian and Egyptian glass was soda ash, sodium carbonate, which can be extracted from the ashes of many plants, notably halophile seashore plants. The earliest vessels were 'core-wound', produced by winding a ductile rope of glass round a shaped core of sand and clay over a metal rod, then fusing it with repeated reheatings. Threads of thin glass of different colours made with admixtures of oxides were subsequently wound around these to create patterns, which could be drawn into festoons by using metal raking tools. The vessel would then be rolled flat ('marvered') on a slab in order to press the decorative threads into its body. Handles and feet were applied separately. The rod was subsequently allowed to cool as the glass slowly annealed and was eventually removed from the centre of the vessel, after which the core material was scraped out. Glass shapes for inlays were also often created in moulds.

Much early glass production, however, relied on grinding techniques borrowed from stone working. This meant that the glass was ground and carved in a cold state.

By the 15th century BC extensive glass production was occurring in Western Asia, Crete and Egypt. It is thought the techniques and recipes required for the initial fusing of glass from raw materials was a closely guarded technological secret reserved for the large palace industries of powerful states. Glass workers in other areas therefore relied on imports of pre-formed glass, often in the form of cast ingots such as those found on the Ulu Burun shipwreck off the coast of Turkey.

Glass remained a luxury material, and the disasters that overtook Late Bronze Age civilisations seem to have brought glass-making to a halt. It picked up again in its former sites, in Syria and Cyprus, in the ninth century BC, when the techniques for making colourless glass were discovered. The first glassmaking 'manual' dates back to ca. 650 BC. Instructions on how to make glass are contained in cuneiform tablets discovered in the library of the Assyrian king Ashurbanipal. In Egypt glass-making did not revive until it was reintroduced in Ptolemaic Alexandria. Core-formed vessels and beads were still widely produced, but other techniques came to the fore with experimentation and technological advancements. During the Hellenistic period many new techniques of glass production were introduced and glass began to be used to make larger pieces, notably table wares. Techniques developed during this period include 'slumping' viscous (but not fully molten) glass over a mould in order to form a dish and 'millefiori' (meaning 'thousand flowers') technique, where canes of multi-coloured glass were sliced and the slices arranged together and fused in a mould to create a mosaic-like effect. It was also during this period that colourless or decoloured glass began to be prized and methods for achieving this effect were investigated more fully.

According to Pliny the Elder, Phoenician traders were the first to stumble upon glass manufacturing techniques at the site of the Belus River. Georgius Agricola, in *De re metallica*, reported a traditional serendipitous 'discovery' tale of familiar type.

"The tradition is that a merchant ship laden with nitrum being moored at this place, the merchants were preparing their meal on the beach, and not having stones to prop up their pots, they used lumps of nitrum from the ship, which fused and mixed with the sands of the shore, and there flowed streams of a new translucent liquid, and thus was the origin of glass."

This account is more a reflection of Roman experience of glass production, however, as white silica sand from this area was used in the production of Roman glass due to its low impurity levels.During the first century BC glass blowing was discovered on the Syro-Palestinian coast, revolutionising the industry and laying the way for the growth of glass production that occurred throughout the Roman world. It was the Romans who began to use glass for architectural purposes, with the discovery of clear glass (through the introduction of manganese oxide), in Alexandria ca. AD 100. Cast glass windows, albeit with poor optical qualities, thus began to appear in the most important buildings in Rome and the most luxurious villas of Herculaneum and Pompeii. Over the next 1,000 years glass making and working continued and spread through southern Europe and beyond.

India (Hindu Kingdoms)

Indigenous development of glass technology in South Asia may have begun in 1730 BCE. Evidence of this culture includes a red-brown glass bead along with a hoard of beads dating to that period, making it the earliest attested glass from the Indus Valley locations. Glass discovered from later sites dating from 600-300 BCE displays common colour.

Chalcolithic evidence of glass has been found in Hastinapur, India. Some of the texts which mention glass in India are the *Shatapatha Brahmana* and *Vinaya Pitaka*. However, the first unmistakable evidence in large quantities, dating from the 3rd century BCE, has been uncovered from the archaeological site in Takshashila, ancient India.

By the first century C.E., glass was being used for ornaments and casing in South Asia. Contact with the Greco-Roman world added newer techniques, and Indians artisans mastered several techniques of glass molding, decorating and colouring by the succeeding centuries. The Satavahana period of India also produced short cylinders of composite glass, including those displaying a lemon yellow matrix covered with green glass.

Glass objects from the 7th and 8th centuries have been found on the island of Torcello near Venice. These form an important link between Roman times and the later importance of that city in the production of the material. Around 1000 AD, an important technical breakthrough was made in Northern Europe when soda glass, produced from white pebbles and burnt vegetation was replaced by glass made from a much more readily available material: potash obtained from wood ashes. From this point on, northern glass differed significantly from that made in the Mediterranean area, where soda remained in common use.

Until the 12th century, stained glass — glass to which metallic or other impurities had been added for colouring — was not widely used, but it rapidly became an important medium for Romanesque art and especially Gothic art. Almost all survivals are in church buildings, but it was also used in grand secular buildings.

The 11th century saw the emergence in Germany of new ways of making sheet glass by blowing spheres. The spheres were swung out to form cylinders and then cut while still hot, after which the sheets were flattened. This technique was perfected in 13th century Venice.

The Crown glass process was used up to the mid-19th century. In this process, the glassblower would spin approximately 9 pounds (4 kg) of molten glass at the end of a rod until it flattened into a disk approximately 5 feet (1.5 m) in diameter. The disk would then be cut into panes.

Murano Glassmaking

The centre for luxury Italian glassmaking from the 14th century was the island of Murano, which developed many new techniques and became the center of a lucrative export trade in dinnerware, mirrors, and other items. What made Venetian Murano glass significantly different was that the local quartz pebbles were almost pure silica, and were ground into a fine clear sand that was combined with soda ash obtained from the Levant, for which the Venetians held the sole monopoly. The clearest and finest glass is tinted in two ways: firstly, a natural colouring agent is ground and melted with the glass. Many of these colouring agents still exist today; for a list of colouring agents, see below. Black glass was called obsidianus after obsidian stone. A second method is apparently to produce a black glass which, when held to the light, will show the true colour that this glass will give to another glass when used as a dye.

The Venetian ability to produce this superior form of glass resulted in a trade advantage over other glass producing lands. Murano's reputation as a centre for glassmaking was born when the Venetian Republic, fearing fire might burn down the city's mostly wood buildings, ordered glassmakers to move their foundries to Murano in 1291. Murano's glassmakers were soon the island's most prominent citizens. Glassmakers were not allowed to leave the Republic. Many took a risk and set up glass furnaces in surrounding cities and as far afield as England and the Netherlands.

From the 19th century, various types of fancy glass started to become significant branches of the decorative arts. Cameo glass was revived for the first time since the Romans, initially mostly used for pieces in a neo-classical style. The Art Nouveau movement in particular made great use of glass, with René Lalique, Émile Gallé, and Daum of Nancy important names in the first French wave of the movement, producing coloured vases and similar pieces, often in cameo glass, and also using lustre techniques. Louis Comfort Tiffany in America specialized in secular stained glass, mostly of plant subjects, both in panels and his famous lamps. From the 20th century, some glass artists began to class themselves as in effect sculptors working in glass, and as part of the fine arts.

Several of the most common techniques for producing glass art include: blowing, kiln-casting, fusing, slumping, pate-de-verre, flame-working, hot-sculpting and cold-working. Cold work includes traditional stained glass work as well as other methods of shaping glass at room temperature. Glass can also be cut with a diamond saw, or copper wheels embedded with abrasives, and polished to give gleaming facets; the technique used in creating Waterford crystal. Art is sometimes etched into glass via the use of acid, caustic, or abrasive substances. Traditionally this was done after the glass was blown or cast. In the 1920s a new mould-etch process was invented, in which art was etched directly into the mould, so that each cast piece emerged from the mould with the image already on the surface of the glass. This reduced manufacturing costs and, combined with a wider use of coloured glass, led to cheap glassware in the 1930s, which later became known as Depression glass. As the types of acids used in this process are extremely hazardous, abrasive methods have gained popularity.

Objects made out of glass include not only traditional objects such as vessels (bowls, vases, bottles, and other containers), paperweights, marbles, beads, but an endless range of sculpture and installation art as well. Coloured glass is often used, though sometimes the glass is painted, innumerable examples exist of the use of stained glass.

Museums

Apart from historical collections in general museums, modern works of art in glass can be seen in a variety of museums, including the Chrysler Museum, the Museum of Glass in Tacoma, the Metropolitan Museum of Art, the Toledo Museum of Art, and Corning Museum of Glass, in Corning, NY, which houses the world's largest collection of glass art and history, with more than 45,000 objects in its collection.

The Harvard Museum of Natural History has a collection of extremely detailed models of flowers made of painted glass. These were lampworked by Leopold Blaschka and his son Rudolph, who never revealed the method he used to make them. The Blaschka Glass Flowers are still an inspiration to glassblowers today.

2

Physics of Glass

The *physics of glass* is the science of the glassy or amorphous state of matter as seen from an atomic or molecular point of view. This article provides an overview of research into glass—a solid in which no significant crystallization has occurred. Thus there is no long-range ordering or extended formation of any Bravais lattice.

Generally speaking, the atomic or molecular structure of glass exists in a metastable state with respect to its crystalline form. That is, glass would convert into a more stable crystalline form, but the rate of this conversion is slow. This essentially reflects the dynamic nature of the glass transition and the formation of the elastic solid from a non-equilibrium supercooled liquid state.

Much work has been done to elucidate the primary microstructural features of glass forming substances at both small (microscopic) and large (macroscopic) scales. One emerging school of thought is that a glass is simply the 'limiting case' of a polycrystalline solid at small crystal size. Within this framework, *domains*, exhibiting various degrees of short-range order, become the building blocks of both metals and alloys, as well as glasses and ceramics. The microstructural defects of both within and between these domains provide the natural sites for atomic diffusion, and the occurrence of viscous flow and plastic deformation in solids.

Since the early theoretical and experimental investigations on polymorphism and the various states of aggregation which can be assumed by a given substance, the glassy (or 'vitreous') state of matter has been recognized as having the mechanical response of both solid and liquid states, depending on the time and length scale under consideration. The primary focus of this article is to understand how these ideas can be implemented within the scope of previous work done regarding the dynamics of the glassy state of matter. After an initial review of the fundamental concepts of viscosity as they pertain to glass-forming liquids, a closer look at the phenomenon of structural or stress relaxation will be augmented by a thorough treatment of much of the experimental work which has been done in the past in order to understand the nature of viscoelastic behaviour and viscous flow, or plastic deformation in solids.

The direction will then turn towards the process of vitrification and the glass transition, where we will begin by noting that the lattice network of a solid can be represented by the superposition of elastic waves of atomic displacement. This description of the lattice structure lends itself naturally to a description of density fluctuations or thermal phonons, whose interactions are described also in the theory of heat transport in both crystalline and non-crystalline solids. The final considerations will be those arising from the differences in the electronic stucture of different glass forming materials.

Domains and Defects

Henry Eyring was among the first to explain the effects of liquid structure on various modes of molecular diffusion. Utilizing the 'hole' or 'free volume' theory of non-associated liquids, Eyring attempted to explain viscosity, plasticity and diffusion in liquids as the formation and filling of molecular-sized holes. In a manner analogous to that proposed by Einstein for a crystalline solid in his theory of specific heat, each atom is regarded as moving independently of all other atoms.

Eyring treated atoms as hard spheres and ascribed a certain 'free volume' to each sphere, corresponding to the volume traced out due to thermal displacements of a particle from its equilibrium position. He accounts for the low entropy of fusion (latent heat divided by fusion temperature) of the alkali metals by assuming that the frequency of the atomic vibrations increases on melting, owing to the volume increase. However, Frenkel pointed out that the average oscillation frequency will be a decreasing function of the volume. A more satisfactory approximation was put forth by Lennard-Jones, who considered used interatomic forces in order to calculate the electric field surrounding a single atom.

Mott and Gurney pointed out the absence in these theories of the concept of a varying degree of atomic or molecular order, suggesting the possibility of a continuous transition from the solid to the liquid phase. Bernal, however, had shown on geometrical grounds with various modes of particle packing that no continuous transition from the crystalline to the amorphous or liquid state is possible without passing through the polycrystalline state, in which regular regions are separated by regions of misfit.

Highlighted image of surface of colloidal solid. Emphasis on microstructural defects to illustrate the defect/ domain morphology typical of a simple one-component glass.

It was therefore proposed that an amorphous solid or glass is nothing more than the limiting state of a polycrystalline solid in which the individual grains or domains are so small that one cannot draw any sharp distinction between the surfaces or misfit. This suggestion was made in the interest of improvement over the interpretation made by Eyring of the entropy of fusion for the liquid state. Thus, the energy of the aggregate is assumed to be proportional to the total area of the surfaces of misfit, and the entropy approximated accordingly. Subsequent papers by Lennard-Jones *et al.* on cooperative phenomena emphasized the order-disorder transition of melting, utilizing the statistical approach of the Bragg–Williams model.

Frenkel formalized the notion of temporary (or temporal) domains in his classical text which includes a description of heterophase density fluctuations. In this context, fluctuations in particle density with configurations resembling that of the crystalline state will exist in a liquid at temperatures above the melting point. An equilibrium distribution of such fluctuations will be in a constant state of growth and dissolution, and will not require the simultaneous collision of the total number of particles in each domain.

Ookawa emphasized the crystallite theory of liquids and its consequences on melting and viscous flow. He points out that the specific heat is one of the macroscopic properties that truly reflects the mode of thermal motion of the primary particles in different states of aggregation. He interprets specific heat measurements as indicating that the thermal agitation of the constituent elements of a liquid is nearly vibrational (solid-like) at low temperature, but almost non-vibrational as high temperature.

Ookawa also showed that the domain size is a decreasing function of temperature. Smaller domains are seen to be strongly coupled with a resulting cooperative motion. In systems with a finite compressibility, the degree of correlations between the displacements of neighbouring crystallites will decrease with the distance of separation. Such correlated displacements are shown to be necessary in the consideration of the dynamic properties of the liquid under a sufficiently large external force.

Furthermore, a constant of proportionality exists (the viscosity) between the rate of shear strain and the applied force in normal Newtonian liquids, and consideration of correlations are unnecessary. But under sufficient external force, the proportionality is lost with non-Newtonian effects becoming manifest. In either case, translational motion at the inter-crystalline boundaries is accompanied by the relative shear movement of the crystallites. The motion of the boundary, which is assumed to be non-directional in the natural state, becomes predominant in one direction in a shear stressed state, resulting in a macroscopic flow of the system.

This interpretation of boundary motion is similar to that of Mott, who suggests that the fluidity of a liquid is due only to the presence of a large number of such mobile crystal defects. Mott's interpretation of melting or loss of rigidity of a polycrystalline mass is therefore based on the point at which boundaries between individual grains can move freely through the aggregate. This is similar to Frenkel's suggestion that the viscous flow of a liquid and its crystallization both take place by the same mechanism of diffusion.

Dislocations and Melting

Kurosawa's study suggested that the contribution of lattice defects is more important than that of lattice vibrations in the melting of ionic crystals. Kuhlmannn-Wilsdorf, emphasizing that the state of a dislocation core is more liquid than solid-like, suggested the pairing of dislocations whose Burgers vectors were of equal magnitude but opposite sign. In this 'dislocation dipole', the long-range strain fields of the two members of the dipole cancel each other, resulting in a loss of all resistance to shear forces.

Consider an elementary dislocation on a triangular lattice. The Burgers vector is the amount by which the path around the singularity fails to close. (The pattern would be a closed circuit on a perfect lattice). The *6 coordinated dislocation* can be broken down into individual *5 and 7 coordinated disclinations* which are all separated by one lattice spacing.

The heterogeneous free volume description (domains *vs.* defects) was considered also by Turnbull and Cohen in order to describe molecular transport in liquids and glasses. Utilizing the free volume model developed by Doolittle to describe viscous flow in Newtonian liquids, a relationship between the diffusion coefficient and the free volume was proposed based upon the concept that statistical redistribution of the free volume occasionally opens up voids large enough for diffusive displacement of a molecule which is typically confined within a molecular cage.

Glass formation occurs when the rate of cooling exceeds the time necessary for such diffusion to occur, thus limiting the molecular motion. This approach has been generalized by Cohen and Grest in the development of a formal treatment of relaxation processes in liquids and glasses. Other defect-diffusion models have also been developed which are based on the proposed existence of one mechanism for relaxation. Thus, at any molecular site, relaxation can only occur when a defect diffuses to the site. This approach has been used in order to describe volume-controlled relaxations in viscoelastic media.

Consider an edge dislocation in a crystal lattice. The Burgers vector is the amount by which the path around the singularity fails to close. The pattern would be a closed circuit on a perfect lattice.

The notion of inter-crystalline or grain boundaries being composed of proper arrays of dislocations led to the next logical step in the sequence of events leading to an understanding of flow mechanisms in liquids as well as in solids. MacKenzie and Mott suggested the possibility that melting results from a sudden proliferation of dislocations.

This led Shockley to establish a relationship between the mobility of a dislocation and the fluidity of a liquid in quantitative manner, by assuming a value for the effective dislocation concentration in the liquid state (combined with certain assumptions regarding dislocation width). Sears subsequently proposed that viscosity anomalies in supercooled liquids result from the growth of solid-like nuclei via a screw dislocation mechanism. Cahn elaborated on the conept of crystal growth from the liquid state by proposing that — in sufficiently supercooled systems — a liquid-solid interface can advance normal to itself in the absence of any such heterogeneities.

Viscoelasticity

Even most simple liquids will exhibit some elastic response at frequencies or shear rates exceeding 5×10^6 Hz. Alternatively, if the vibrational period of the force is large (low frequency) compared with the relaxation time, then the vibrational motion of the body will partially degenerate into translational motion, and the resulting displacement will be evidenced by viscous flow. Materials which respond to mechanical disturbances by both viscous (or plastic/irreversible) and elastic (or reversible) behaviour under distinct ranges of deformation (and rate deformation, or frequency) are referred to as viscoelastic.

Thus, when a mechanical force is applied suddenly to a fluid, the fluid responds elastically at first, just as if it were a solid body. Whether the rigidity or the fluidity predominates in a material under given conditions is therefore determined by the time scale of the experiment relative to the characteristic time of structural relaxation of the material. Zwanzig and Mountain calculated the high-frequency elastic moduli of simple fluids by considering the pressure and internal energy of the fluid. They concluded that the initial response to a sudden disturbance can be characterized by two quantities:

1. The high-frequency limit of the shear modulus G (or modulus of rigidity).
2. The high-frequency limit of the bulk modulus K (or modulus of compression).

The connection between a viscous and an elastic response is made by considering the stress for a disturbance varying periodically in time with a frequency,?. For consideration of shear flow, it is supposed that the shear viscosity *q*(?) is a function of the frequency, and is related to the relaxation time *t*, which is characteristic of the transition from elastic to viscous response. High-frequency disturbances are identified as those relating to elastic behaviour, while low-frequency behaviour is identified as ordinary viscous flow. Thus the frequency-dependent viscosity coefficient *q*(?) is capable of describing both viscous and elastic phenomena, and can be related to the frequency-dependent elastic moduli, *K*(?) and *G*(?).

In the study of the high-frequency dynamics of simple liquids and solids near their melting points, the particular condition of zero vibrational frequency has been referred to as the 'thermodynamic limit' (? ? 0). The conclusions of inelastic light scattering studies near the melting point is that there is no discernible difference between the liquid and solid vibrational spectra at sufficiently high frequencies. Thus, on the short time and length scales probed by these experiments, melting causes no discontinuous change in the microscopic dynamics of the substance. The lower the frequency, the larger the discontinuity between liquid and solid behaviour — so that in the thermodynamic limit (zero frequency) the transition is first order.

Vitrification

Early Work

Since the early theoretical and experimental investigations on polymorphism and the various states of aggregation which can be assumed by a given substance, the vitreous state of a substance has been recognized as having the mechanical response of both solid and liquid, depending on the time and spatial scale under consideration. The atomic arrangement of network-forming oxides in the vitreous or glassy state was initially described as exhibiting the disorder (or short-range order) of its liquid precursor and therefore defying description through any crystalline hypotheses.

A multitude of substances including polymers, network forming oxides, and metallic alloys exhibit glass-forming characteristics, and it is of interest to discuss the criterion which separates the glass forming ability from the typically observed nucleation and growth of a crystalline phase.

It was initially suggested that the ultimate condition for the formation of a glass is that the substance can form extended three-dimensional networks lacking periodicity with an energy content comparable with that of the corresponding crystal network. Viscous flow characteristics of liquids near the glass transition temperature T_g were then interpreted in terms of configurational changes at the molecular level.

Other authors pointed out that the metastable nature of the glassy state is associated with the freezing-in of certain internal degrees of freedom in the liquid, and proceeded to formalize a treatment of the thermodynamics and kinetics of the irreversible approach to equilibrium in glasses in terms of such macroscopic thermodynamic variables as the volume, enthalpy and entropy. Such treatments led to controversy over the use of irreversible thermodynamics in the treatment of glass formation, and the order (first or second) of the macroscopic phase transition. Such questions remain highly controversial in scientific circles today.

The difficulties involved in developing a fundamental understanding of the nature of the glass transition itself are similar to those involved in the understanding of any rate-controlled phenomena, such as chemical reactions. A distinction should be drawn between an empirical description of the kinetics of the reaction and a description in terms of its macroscopic variables (enthalpy, entropy, etc.), and a physical understanding of the reaction itself. The latter involves a picture of its mechanism, i.e., the path of the reaction.

This point is emphasized in a dynamic interpretation of vitrification. Thus, the kinetic treatment of glass formation by Uhlmann which is based upon the kinetic equations for phase changes developed by Avrami should be contrasted, for example, with a mechanical description of vitrification. The latter emphasizes the localized nature of the distribution of microscopic stress and strain upon vitrification.

Elastic Waves

Thus, it may be wise to note that the dynamics of any rate-controlled phenomena can only be understood if one considers the dynamic nature of its primary constituents. In this particular case, thermal motion in liquids can be decomposed into elementary longitudinal waves (or acoustic phonons), while transverse waves (or shear waves) were originally described (and observed) only in the crystalline state. This is the fundamental reason why simple liquids cannot support a shearing stress, but rather yield via plastic deformation and macroscopic flow. The inadequacies of this conclusion, however, were pointed out by Frenkel in his revision of the theory of elasticity of liquids. This revision follows directly from the continuous character of the transition from the liquid state into the solid one when this transition is not accompanied by crystallization and long-range atomic and/or molecular ordering (or self-assembly).

It can be concluded from these observations on continuity that transverse vibrations can be propagated not only in crystalline bodies, but also in liquids. The fact that this conclusion is not verified experimentally in the case of ordinary liquids is due to the short time scale of relaxation compared to the period of vibrations which can be obtained with the help of modern opto-acoustic methods: lasers and ultrasonics. Under such conditions, the transverse vibrations must be strongly damped.

Experimental verification of these conclusions have been obtained using molecular dynamics computer simulation studies in monatomic liquids and glasses where it has been shown that, at short wavelengths, monatomic liquids can support a propagating shear wave, i.e. a collective excitation which is analogous to the transverse phonons found in solids. The onset of this viscoelastic behaviour is linked to the fact that as the wave number increases the rigidity of the liquid becomes an important factor.

Mechanisms of attenuation of high-frequency shear modes and longitudinal waves were considered with viscous liquids, polymers and glasses. The subsequent work led to a fresh interpretation of the glass transition in viscous liquids in terms of a spectrum of structural relaxation phenomena occurring over a wide range of spatial and temporal scales. Experimentally, the use of dynamic light scattering experiments (or photon correlation spectroscopy) allows to study molecular processes down to time intervals of 10^{-11} sec. This is equivalent to extending the available frequency range to 10^9 Hz or greater.

Thus we see the intimate correlation between transverse acoustic phonons (or shear waves) and the onset of rigidity or vitrification. The frequency dependence of this phenomenon becomes apparent when one considers the increasing wavelength over which such rigidity can be observed. The relationship between these transverse waves and the mechanism of vitrification has been described by Chen *et al.* who proposed that the onset of correlations between such phonons results in an orientational ordering or 'freezing' of local shear stresses in liquids, yielding the glass transition.

The representation of thermal motion in liquids as a superposition of elastic sound waves was first introduced by Brillouin. Atomic motion in condensed matter can therefore be represented by a Fourier series of standing waves whose physical interpretation consists of a superposition of supersonic longitudinal and transverse atomic displacement waves (or density fluctuations) with varying directions and wavelengths. With respect to sound wave propagation, the speed of longitudinal or compression waves will be limited by the bulk modulus of compressibility. The square root of the ratio of the bulk modulus K to the density p will be equal to the velocity of propagation of longitudinal phonons. In the case of transverse vibrations or shear waves, for which the density remains constant, the speed of such waves will be limited by the shear modulus or rigidity.

Heat Transport

The velocities of longitudinal acoustic phonons in condensed matter are directly responsible for the thermal conductivity which levels out temperature differentials between compressed and expanded volume elements. The thermal properties of glass are interpreted in terms of an approximately constant mean free path for lattice phonons. Furthermore, the value of the mean free path is of the order of magnitude of the scale of structural (dis)order at the atomic or molecular level.

Thus, heat transport in both glassy and crystalline dielectric solids occurs through elastic vibrations of the lattice. This transport is limited by elastic scattering of acoustic phonons by lattice defects. These predictions were confirmed by the experiments of Chang and Jones on commercial glasses and glass ceramics, where mean free paths were limited by 'internal boundary scattering' to length scales of 10^{-2} cm to 10^{-3} cm.

The phonon mean free path has been associated directly with the effective relaxation length for processes without directional correlation. Thus, if V_g is the group velocity of a phonon wave packet, then the relaxation length is defined as:

where *t* is the characteristic relaxation time. Now, since longitudinal waves have a much greater group or 'phase velocity' than that of transverse waves, V_{long} is much greater than V_{trans}, the relaxation length or mean free path of longitudinal phonons will be much greater. Thus, thermal conductivity will be largely determined by the speed of longitudinal phonons.

Regarding the dependence of wave velocity on wavelength or frequency (aka 'dispersion'), low-frequency phonons of long wavelength will be limited in relaxation length by elastic Rayleigh scattering. This type of light scattering form small partilces is proportional to the fourth power of the frequency. For higher frequencies, the power of the frequency will decrease until at highest frequencies scattering is almost frequency independent. Such higher frequency phonons may be scattered by 'defect clusters'.

Similar arguments were subsequently generalized to many glass forming substances using Brillouin scattering (thermal generation of phonons with detection by light scattering).

Some experiments have been contrasted with these theories interpreting thermal resistance as being due to scattering of sound waves by lattice defects in crystals. Diffuse scattering of phonons has been attributed rather to the general 'roughness' of the amorphous structure which is said not to contain such well defined lattice defects.

The thermal phonon mean free paths or relaxation lengths of a number of glass formers have been plotted *versus* the glass transition temperature, indicating a linear relationship between the two. This has suggested a new criterion for glass formation based on the value of the phonon mean free path.

Electronic Structure

The influence of thermal phonons and their interaction with electronic structure is a topic which was appropriately introduced in a disussion of the resistance of liquid metals. Lindemann's theory of melting is referenced, and it is suggested that the drop in conductivity in going from the crystalline to the liquid state is due to the increased scattering of conduction electrons as a result of the increased amplitude of atomic vibration. Such theories of localization have been applied to transport in metallic glasses, where the mean free path of the electrons is very small (on the order of the interatomic spacing).

The formation of a non-crystalline form of a gold-silicon alloy by the method of splat quenching from the melt led to further considerations of the influence of electronic structure on glass forming ability based on the properties of the metallic bond.

Other work indicates that the mobility of localized electrons is enhanced by the presence of dynamic phonon modes. One claim against such a model is that if chemical bonds are important, the nearly free electron models should not be applicable. However, if the model includes the build-up of a charge distribution between all pairs of atoms just like a chemical bond (e.g., silicon, when a band is just filled with electrons) then it should apply to solids.

Thus, if the electrical conductivity is low, the mean free path of the electrons is very short. The electrons will only be sensitive to the short-range order in the glass since they do not get a chance to scatter from atoms spaced at large distances. Since the short-range order is similar in glasses and crystals, the electronic energies should be similar in these two states. For alloys with lower resistivity and longer electronic mean free paths, the electrons could begin to sense that there is disorder in the glass, and this would raise their energies and destabilize the glass with respect to crystallization. Thus, the glass formation tendencies of certain alloys may therefore be due in part to the fact that the electron mean free paths are very short, so that only the short-range order is ever important for the energy of the electrons.

Other authors have suggested that the electronic structure yields its influence on glass formation through the directional properties of bonds. Non-crystallinity is thus favoured in elements with a large number of polymorphic forms and a high degree of bonding anisotropy. Crystallization becomes more unlikely as bonding anisotropy is increased from isotropic metallic to anisotropic metallic to covalent bonding, thus suggesting a relationship between the group number in the periodic table and the glass forming ability in elemental solids.

3

Glass Transition

Glass transition or *vitrification* refers to the transformation of a glass-forming liquid into a glass, which usually occurs upon rapid cooling. It is a dynamic phenomenon occurring between two distinct states of matter (liquid and glass), each with different physical properties. Upon cooling through the temperature range of glass transition (a 'glass transformation range'), without forming any long-range order or significant symmetry of atomic arrangement, the liquid contracts more continuously at about the same rate as above the melting point until there is a decrease in the thermal expansion coefficient (TEC).

The glass transition temperature, T_g, is lower than melting temperature, T_m, due to supercooling. It depends on the time scale of observation which must be defined by convention. One approach is to agree on a standard cooling rate of 10 K/min. Another approach is by requiring a viscosity of 10^{13} poise. Otherwise, one can only talk about a glass transformation range.

The glassy or vitreous state of matter is typically formed by rapid cooling and solidification from the molten (or liquid) state. If the liquid were allowed to crystallize on cooling, then according to the Ehrenfest classification of first-order phase transitions, there would be a discontinuous change in volume (and thus a discontinuity in the slope or first derivative with respect to temperature, dV/dT) at the melting point. In this context, glass and melt are distinct phases with an interfacial discontinuity having a surface of tension with a positive surface energy. Thus, a metastable parent phase is always stable with respect to the nucleation of small embryos or droplets from a daughter phase, provided it has a positive surface of tension. Such first-order transitions must proceed by the advancement of an interfacial region whose structure and properties vary discontinuously from the parent phase.

Below the transition temperature range, the glassy structure does not relax in accordance with the cooling rate used. The expansion coefficient for the glassy state is roughly equivalent to that of the crystalline solid. If slower cooling rates are used, the increased time for structural relaxation (or intermolecular rearrangement) to occur may result in a higher density glass product. Similarly, by annealing (and thus allowing for slow structural relaxation) the glass structure in time approaches an equilibrium density corresponding to the supercooled liquid at this same temperature. T_g is located at the intersection between the cooling curve (volume versus temperature) for the glassy state and the supercooled liquid.

The configuration of the glass in this temperature range changes slowly with time towards the equilibrium structure. The principle of the minimization of the Gibbs free energy provides the thermodynamic driving force necessary for the eventual change. It should be noted here that at somewhat higher temperatures than T_g, the structure corresponding to equilibrium at any temperature is achieved quite rapidly. In contrast, at considerably lower temperatures, the configuration of the glass remains sensibly stable over increasingly extended periods of time.

Thus, the liquid-glass transition is not a transition between states of thermodynamic equilibrium. It is widely believed that the true equilibrium state is always crystalline. Glass is believed to exist in a metastable state, and its entropy, density, and so on, depend on the thermal history.

Therefore, the glass transition is primarily a dynamic phenomenon. Time and temperature are interchangeable quantities (to some extent) when dealing with glasses, a fact often expressed in the time-temperature superposition principle. On cooling a liquid, *internal degrees of freedom successively fall out of equilibrium.* However, there is a longstanding debate whether there is an underlying second-order phase transition in the hypothetical limit of infinitely long relaxation times.

Ideal glass formers are typically composed of molecular networks whose intricate geometries do not lend themselves easily to long-range order formation and higher orders of symmetry. In the vast majority of silicates, the *Si* atom shows tetrahedral coordination, with 4 oxygen atoms surrounding a central *Si* atom.

All but one of the crystalline forms involve tetrahedral SiO_4 units linked together by shared vertices in different arrangements. In different minerals the tetrahedra show different degrees of networking and polymerization. For example, they occur singly, joined together in pairs, in larger finite clusters including rings, in chains, double chains, sheets, and three-dimensional frameworks. The minerals are classified into groups based on these structures.

The most common example is seen in the quartz crystalline form of silicon dioxide, or silica SiO_2. In each of the most thermodynamically stable crystalline forms of silica, on average, only 2 out of 4 of each the vertices (or oxygen atoms) of the SiO_4 tetrahedra are shared with others, yielding the net chemical formula: SiO_2. For example, in the unit cell of alpha-quartz, the central tetrahedron shares all 4 of its corner *O* atoms, the 2 face-centred tetrahedra share 2 of their corner O atoms, and the 4 edge-centered tetrahedra share just 1 of their *O* atoms with other SiO_4 tetrahedra. This leaves a net average of 12 out of 24 (or 1 out of 2) total vertices for that portion of the 7 SiO_4 tetrahedra which are considered to be a part of the unit cell for silica.

The amorphous structure of glassy silica (SiO_2). No long-range order is present, however there is local ordering with respect to the tetrahedral arrangement of oxygen (O) atoms around the silicon (Si) atoms.

Silica (the chemical compound SiO_2) has a number of distinct crystalline forms in addition to the quartz structure. Nearly all of the crystalline forms involve tetrahedral SiO_4 units linked together by *shared vertices* in different arrangements. *Si-O* bond lengths vary between the different crystal forms. For example, in a-quartz the bond length is 161 pm, whereas in a-tridymite it ranges from 154-171 pm. The *Si-O-Si* bond angle also varies from 140° in a-tridymite to 144° in a-quartz to 180° in ß-tridymite. Any deviations from these standard parameters constitute microstructural differences or variations which represent an approach to an amorphous, vitreous or glassy solid.

Fluoride glass is a class of non-oxide optical quality glasses composed of fluorides of various metals. Due to their low viscosity, it is very difficult to completely avoid the occurrence of any crystallization while processing it through the glass transition (or drawing the fibre from the melt). Thus, although heavy metal fluoride glasses (HMFG) exhibit very low optical attenuation, they are not only difficult to manufacture, but are quite fragile, and have poor resistance to moisture and other environmental attacks. Their best attribute is that they lack the absorption band associated with the hydroxyl (OH) group (3200-3600 cm^{-1}) which is present in nearly all oxide-based glasses.

An example of a heavy metal fluoride glass is the ZBLAN glass group, composed of zirconium, barium, lanthanum, aluminum, and sodium fluorides. Their main technological application is as optical waveguides in both planar and fibre form. They are advantageous especially in the mid-infrared (2-5 μm) range.

HMFG's were initially slated for optical fibre applications, because the intrinsic losses of a mid-IR fibre could in principle be lower than those of silica fibres, which are transparent only up to ~ 2?µm. However, such low losses were never realized in practice, and the fragility and high cost of fluoride fibres made them less than ideal as primary candidates. Later, the utility of fluoride fibres for various other applications was discovered. These include mid-IR spectroscopy, fibre-optic sensors, thermometry, and imaging. Also, fluoride fibres can be used to for guided lightwave transmission in media such as YAG (ytrria-alumina garnet) lasers at 2.9?µm, as required for medical applications (e.g. ophthalmology and dentistry).

Phosphates

Phosphate glass constitutes a class of optical glasses composed of metaphosphates of various metals. Instead of the SiO_4 tetrahedra observed in silicate glasses, the building block for this glass former is P_2O_5, which crystallizes in at least four forms. The most familiar polymorph comprises molecules of P_4O_{10}. The other polymorphs are polymeric, but in each case the phosphorus atoms are bound by a tetrahedron of oxygen atoms, one of which forms a terminal $P=O$ bond. The *O*-form adopts a layered structure consisting of interconnected P_6O_6 rings, not unlike the structure adopted by certain polysilicates.

Iron phosphate and lead iron phosphate glass provide alternatives to borosilicate glass for the immobilization of radioactive waste. Phosphate glasses can also be advantageous over silica glasses for optical fibres with high concentration of doping rare earth ions. A mix of fluoride glass and phosphate glass is fluorophosphate glass.

Chalcogenides

The chalcogens — the elements in group VI of the periodic table, particularly sulphur (*S*), selenium (*Se*) and tellurium (*Te*) — react with more electropositive elements, such as silver, to form chalcogenides. These are extremly versatile compounds, in that they can be crystalline or amorphous, metallic or semiconducting, and conductors of ions or electrons. Already important in optical storage discs and fibres, they are now being proposed as the basis for solid-state memory technologies. Moreover, chalcogenide glass materials form the basis of CD and DVD technologies.

Subsequent rapid cooling then sends the melted region back through the glass transition. Conversely, a lower-intensity heat pulse of longer duration will crystallize an amorphous region.

Attempts to induce the glassy–crystal transformation of chalcogenides by electrical means form the basis of phase-change random-access memory (PC-RAM). This emerging technology is on the brink of commercial application by ECD Ovonics. For write operations, an electric current supplies the heat pulse. The read process is performed at sub-threshold voltages by utilizing the relatively large difference in electrical resistance between the glassy and crystalline states. Examples of such phase change materials are *GeSbTe* and *AgInSbTe*. In optical discs, the phase change layer is usually sandwiched between dielectric layers of $ZnS\text{-}SiO_2$. Other less common such materials are *InSe*, *SbSe*, *SbTe*, *InSbSe*, *InSbTe*, *GeSbSe*, *GeSbTeSe*, and *AgInSbSeTe*.

Although the electronic structural transitions relevant to both optical discs and PC-RAM were featured strongly, contributions from ions were not considered — even though amorphous chalcogenides can have significant ionic conductivities. At Euromat 2005, however, it was shown that ionic transport can also be useful for data storage in a solid chalcogenide electrolyte. At the nanoscale, this electrolyte consists of crystalline metallic islands of silver selenide (Ag_2Se) dispersed in an amorphous semiconducting matrix of germanium selenide (Ge_2Se3).

All of these technologies present exciting opportunities that are not restricted to memory, but include cognitive computing and reconfigurable logic circuits. It is too early to tell which technology will be selected for which applicaiotn. But scientific interest alone should drive the continuing research. For example, the migration of dissolved ions is required in the electrolytic case, but could limit the performance of a phase-change device. Diffusion of both electrons and ions participate in electromigration — widely studied as a degradation mechanism of the electrical conductors used in modern integrated circuits. Thus, a unified approach to the study of chalcogenides, assessing the collective roles of atoms, ions and electrons, may prove essential for both device performance and reliability.

Amorphous Metals

In the past, small batches of amorphous metals with high surface area configurations (ribbons, wires, films, etc.) have been produced through the implementation of extremely rapid rates of cooling. This was initially termed 'splat cooling' by Doctoral student W. Klement at Caltech, who showed that cooling rates on the order of millions of degrees per second is sufficient to impede the formation of crystals, and the metallic atoms becomes 'locked into' a glassy state. Amorphous metal wires have been produced by sputtering molten metal onto a spinning metal disk. More recently a number of alloys have been produced in layers with thickness exceeding 1 millimeter. These are known as bulk metallic glasses (BMG). Liquidmetal Technologies sell a number of titanium-based BMGs. Batches of amorphous steel have also been produced that demonstrate mechanical properties far exceeding those found in conventional steel alloys.

In 2004, NIST researchers presented evidence that an isotropic non-crystalline metallic phase (dubbed 'q-glass') could be grown from the melt. This phase is the first phase, or 'primary phase', to form in the *Al-Fe-Si* system during rapid cooling. Interestingly, experimental evidence indicates that this phase forms by a *first-order transition.* Transmission electron microscopy (TEM) images show that the *q*-glass nucleates from the melt as discrete particles, which grow spherically with a uniform growth rate in all directions. The diffraction pattern shows it to be an isotropic glassy phase. Yet there is a nucleation barrier, which implies an interfacial discontinuity (or internal surface) between the glass and the melt.

In polymers the glass transition temperature, T_g, is often expressed as the temperature at which the Gibbs free energy is such that the activation energy for the cooperative movement of 50 or so elements of the polymer is exceeded (reference required). This allows molecular chains to slide past each other when a force is applied. From this definition, we can see that the introduction of relatively stiff chemical groups (such as benzene rings) will interfere with the flowing process and hence increase T_g.

The stiffness of thermoplastics decreases due to this effect. When the glass temperature has been reached, the stiffness stays the same for a while, i.e., at or near E_2, until the temperature exceeds T_m, and the material melts. This region is called the rubber plateau.

In ironing, a fabric is heated through this transition so that the polymer chains become mobile. The weight of the iron then imposes a preferred orientation. T_g can be significantly decreased by addition of plasticizers into the polymer matrix. Smaller molecules of plasticizer embed themselves between the polymer chains, increasing the spacing and free volume, and allowing them to move past one another even at lower temperatures. The 'new-car smell' is due to the initial outgassing of volatile small-molecule plasticizers used to modify interior plastics (e.g., dashboards) to keep them from cracking in the cold, winter weather. The addition of non-reactive side groups to a polymer can also make the chains stand off from one another, reducing T_g. If a plastic with some desirable properties has a T_g which is too high, it can sometimes be combined with another in a copolymer or composite material with a T_g below the temperature of intended use. Note that some plastics are used at high temperatures, e.g., in automobile engines, and others at low temperatures.

In viscoelastic materials, the presence of liquid-like behaviour depends on the properties of and so varies with rate of applied load, i.e., how quickly a force is applied. The silicone toy 'Silly Putty' behaves quite differently depending on the time rate of applying a force: pull slowly and it flows, acting as a heavily viscous liquid; hit it with a hammer and it shatters, acting as a glass.

On cooling, rubber undergoes a *liquid-glass transition*, which has also been called a *rubber-glass transition*. For example, the Space Shuttle Challenger disaster was caused by rubber *O*-rings that were being used well below their glass transition temperature on an unusually cold Florida morning, and thus could not flex adequately to form proper seals between sections of the two solid-fuel rocket boosters.

Biomaterials

When sucrose is cooled slowly, the result is crystal sugar (or rock candy), but, when cooled rapidly, the result can be in the form of syrupy cotton candy (candyfloss).

Vitrification can also occur when starting with a liquid such as water, usually through very rapid cooling or the introduction of agents that suppress the formation of ice crystals. Additives used in cryobiology or produced naturally by organisms living in polar regions are called cryoprotectants. Arctic frogs and some other ectotherms naturally produce glycerol or glucose in their livers to reduce ice formation. When glucose is used as a cryoprotectant by Arctic frogs, massive amounts of glucose are released at low temperature, and a special form of insulin allows for this extra glucose to enter the cells. When the frog rewarms during spring, the extra glucose must be rapidly removed from the cells and recycled via renal excretion and storage in the bladder. Arctic insects also use sugars as cryoprotectants. Arctic fish use antifreeze proteins, sometimes appended with sugars, as cryoprotectant.

Vitrification technology is being used to cryopreserve cells, tissues and organs for transplantation. For years, glycerol has been used in cryobiology as a cryoprotectant for blood cells and bull sperm, allowing storage at liquid nitrogen temperatures. However, glycerol cannot be used to protect whole organs from damage. Instead, many biotechnology companies are currently researching the development of other cryoprotectants more suitable for such uses. A successful discovery may eventually make possible the bulk cryogenic storage (or 'banking') of transplantable human and xenobiotic organs. A substantial step in that direction has already occurred. At the July 2005 annual conference of the Society for Cryobiology, Twenty-First Century Medicine announced the vitrification of a rabbit kidney to -135 °C with their proprietary vitrification cocktail. Upon rewarming, the kidney was successfully transplanted into a rabbit, with complete functionality and viability.

In the context of cryonics, especially in preservation of the human brain, vitrification of tissue is thought to be necessary to prevent destruction of the tissue or information encoded in the brain. At present, vitrification techniques have only been applied to brains (neurovitrification) by Alcor and to the upper body by the Cryonics Institute, but research is in progress by both organizations to apply vitrification to the whole body.

The scientific basis behind the cryonics is that proteins possess a glass transition temperature below which both anharmonic motions and long-range correlated motion within a single molecule are quenched. The origin of this transition is primarily due to 'caging' by glassy water , but can also be modeled in the absence of explicit water molecules, suggesting that part of the transition is due to internal protein dynamics.

Glass-ceramics

Glass-ceramic materials share many properties with both non-crystalline glass and crystalline ceramics. They are formed as a glass, and then partially crystallized by heat treatment. For example, the microstructure of whiteware ceramics frequently contains both amorphous and crystalline phases. Crystalline grains are often embedded within a non-crystalline intergranular phase of grain boundaries. When applied to whiteware ceramics, vitreous means the material has an extremely low permeability to liquids, often but not always water, when determined by a specified test regime.

The term mainly refers to a mix of lithium and aluminosilicates which yields an array of materials with interesting thermomechanical properties. The most commercially important of these have the distinction of being impervious to thermal shock. Thus, glass-ceramics have become extremely useful for countertop cooking. The negative thermal expansion coefficient (TEC) of the crystalline ceramic phase can be balanced with the positive TEC of the glassy phase. At a certain point (~70% crystalline) the glass-ceramic has a net TEC near zero. This type of glass-ceramic exhibits excellent mechanical properties and can sustain repeated and quick temperature changes up to 1000°C.

Vitrification may also occur naturally when lightning strikes the crystalline (e.g. quartz) grains found in most beach sand. In this case, the extreme and immediate heat of the lightning (~2500°C) creates hollow, branching rootlike structures called fulgurite via fusion. Thus, fulgurite tubes have a glassy interior due to rapid cooling and solidification of the crystalline sand after the lightning strike. The size and length of the fulgurite depends on the strength of the lightning strike and the thickness of the sand bed. Many sand fulgurites average 1 or 2 inches (2.5-5 cm) in diameter and can be up to 30 inches (75 cm) long.

Colloidal Glasses

Electron micrograph of surface of colloidal glass. Structure and morphology consist of short-range order with both interdomain and intradomain lattice defects.

A colloidal crystal is a highly ordered array of colloidal particles which can be formed over a very long range (from a few millimetres to one centimeter) in length, and which appear analogous to their atomic or molecular counterparts. One of the finest natural examples of this phenomenon can be found in precious opal, where brilliant regions of pure spectral colour result from close-packed domains of colloidal spheres of amorphous silicon dioxide (or silica, SiO_2).

Thus, it has been known for many years that, due to repulsive Coulombic interactions, electrically charged macromolecules in an aqueous environment can exhibit long-range crystal-like correlations with separation between the particles often being considerably greater than the individual particle diameter. Colloidal solids (both crystals and glasses) are receiving increased attention, largely due to their mechanisms of solidification and self-assembly, cooperative motion, structures similar to those observed in condensed matter (liquids, crystals and glasses) and structural phase transitions including the glass transition. Phase equilibrium has been considered within the context of their physical similarities (with appropriate scaling) to classical elastic solids. In contrast to atomic systems, however, the length or spatial scale is mesoscopic and determined by the spacing between the particles (the cube root of the particle concentration or vol% solids). Thus, colloidal crystals can also exhibit the microstructure of a glass-like amorphous solid on an appropriately larger spatial scale. Concentrated colloidal suspensions may exhibit a distinct glass transition as function of particle concentration or density.

4

Porous Glass

Porous glass is glass that includes pores, usually in the nm- or µm-range, commonly prepared by one of the following processes:

1. metastable phase separation in borosilicate glasses (such as in the system SiO_2-B_2O_3-Na_2O), followed by liquid extraction of one of the formed phases;
2. the sol-gel process; or
3. simply by sintering glass powder.

The specific properties and commercial availability of porous glass make it one of the most extensively researched and characterized amorphous solids. Due to the possibility of modelling the microstructure, porous glasses have a high potential as a model system. They show a high chemical, thermal and mechanical resistance, which results from a rigid and incompressible silica network. They can be produced in high quality and with pore sizes ranging from 1 nm up to any desired value. An easy functionalization of the inner surface opens a wide field of applications for porous glasses.

A further special advantage of porous glasses compared to other porous materials is that they can be made not only as powder or granulate, but also as larger pieces in almost any user defined shape and texture.

In the first half of the 20th century, Turner and Winks discovered that borosilicate glasses can be leached by acids. Their investigations showed that not only the chemical stability can be influenced by thermal treatment but also density, refractive index, thermal expansion and viscosity. In 1934, Nordberg and Hood discovered that alkali borosilicate glasses separate in soluble (sodium borate rich) and insoluble (silica rich) phases if the glass is thermally treated. By extraction using mineral acids the soluble phase can be removed and a porous silica network remains. During a sintering process after extraction, a silica glass is generated, which has properties approaching those of quartz glass. The manufacturing of such high-silica glasses has been published as VYCOR-process.

Definition

In the scientific literature, porous glass is a porous material containing approximately 96 per cent silica, which is produced by an acidic extraction or a combined acidic and alkaline extraction respectively of phase separated alkali borosilicate glasses and features a three-dimensional interconnected porous microstructure. For commercially available porous glasses, the terms porous VYCOR-Glass (PVG) and Controlled Pore Glass (CPG) are used. The pore structure is formed by a syndetic channel system and has a specific surface from 10 to 300 m^2/g. Porous glasses can be generated by an acidic extraction of phase separated alkaliborosilica glasses or by a sol-gel-process. By regulating the manufacturing parameters, it is possible to produce a porous glass with a pore size between 0.4 and 1000 nm in a very narrow pore size distribution. You can generate various moulds, for example irregular particles (powder, granulate), spheres, plates, sticks, fibres, ultra thin membranes, tubes, and rings.

Precondition for repetitious manufacturing of porous glass is the knowledge about structure determining and structure controlling parameters. The composition of the initial glass is a structure controlling parameter. The manufacturing of the initial glass, mainly the cooling process, the temperature and time of thermal treatment, and the after treatment are structure determining parameters. The phase diagram for sodiumborosilica glass shows a miscibility gap for certain glass compositions.

The upper critical temperature lies at about 760°C and the lower one at about 500°C. O.S. Moltschanova was the first person who exactly described the definition of the exsolution. For a phase separation the initial glass composition must lie in the miscibility gap of the ternary Na_2-B_2O_3-SiO_2-glass system. By a thermal treatment, an interpenetration structure is generated, which results from a spinodal decomposition of the sodium-rich borate phase and the silica phase. This procedure is called primary decomposition. Using an initial glass composition, which lies on the line of anomaly, you get a maximum decomposition, which is almost strainless.

As both phases have a different resistances to water, mineral acids, and inorganic salt solutions, you can remove the sodium-rich borate phase in these mediums by extraction. Optimal extraction is possible only if the initial glass composition and thermal treatment are chosen such that combine structures form, and not droplet structures. The texture is influenced by the composition of the initial glass, which directs size and type of decomposition areas. In the context of porous glasses, "texture" implies properties like specific pore volume, specific surface, pore size, and porosity. The emerging areas of decomposition depend on time and temperature of the thermal treatment. Furthermore, the texture of porous glasses is influenced by the concentration of the extraction medium and the ratio of fluid to solid.

Also colloidal silica is solving in the sodium-rich borate phase, when time and temperature of thermal treatment are increased. This process is called secondary decomposition.

The colloidal silica deposit in the macro pores during extraction and obscure the real pore structure. The solubility of colloidal silica in alkaline solutions is higher than network silica, and thus can be removed by an alkaline after-treatment.

Applications

Because of their high mechanical, thermal, and chemical stability, variable manufacturing of pore sizes with a small pore size distribution and variety of surface modifications, a wide array of applications are possible. The fact that porous glasses can be produced in many different shapes is another advantage for application in industry, medicine, pharmacy research, biotechnology, and sensor technology.

Porous glasses are ideal for material separation, because of the small pore size distribution. This is why they are used in gas chromatography, thin layer chromatography, and affinity chromatography. An adaptation of stationary phase for a separation problem is possible by a specific modification of the surface of the porous glass.

In biotechnology, porous glasses have benefits for the cleaning of DNA and the immobilization of enzymes or microorganisms. They are also excellently suited for the synthesis of oligonucleotides. For this, special startnucleotides are mustered on the inner surface. The chain length of produced oligonucleotides is influenced by the pore size of the glass.

In addition, porous glasses are used for manufacturing implants, especially dental implants, for which porous glass powder is processed with plastics to form a composite. The particle size and the pore size influence the elasticity of the composite so as to fit the optical and mechanical properties to surrounding tissue, e.g. the appearance and hardness of dental enamel.

With the ability to form porous glasses as platelets, membrane technology is another important area of application. Hyper filtration of sea- and brackish water and ultra filtration in 'downstream process' are but two. Additionally, they are often appropriate as a carrier in catalysts. For example, the Olefin — metathesis was realized on the system metal — metal oxide/porous glass.

Porous glasses can be used as membrane reactors as well, again because of their high mechanical, thermal, and chemical stability. Membrane reactors can improve conversion of limited balance reactions, while one reaction product is removed by a selective membrane. For example, in the decomposition of hydrogen sulfide on a catalyst in a glass capillary, the conversion by reaction was higher with glass capillary than without.

5

Sol-Gel

The *sol-gel* process, also known as chemical solution deposition, is a wet-chemical technique widely used in the fields of materials science and ceramic engineering. Such methods are used primarily for the fabrication of materials (typically a metal oxide) starting from a chemical solution which acts as the precursor for an integrated network (or *gel*) of either discrete particles or network polymers. Typical precursors are metal alkoxides and metal chlorides, which undergo various forms of hydrolysis and polycondensation reactions. The formation of a metal oxide involves connecting the metal centres with oxo (M-O-M) or hydroxo (M-OH-M) bridges, therefore generating metal-oxo or metal-hydroxo polymers in solution. Thus, the sol evolves towards the formation of a gel-like diphasic system containing both a liquid phase and solid phase whose morphologies range from discrete particles to continuous polymer networks.

In the case of the colloid, the volume fraction of particles (or particle density) may be so low that a significant amount of fluid may need to be removed initially for the gel-like properties to be recognized. This can be accomplished in any number of ways. The most simple method is to allow time for sedimentation to occur, and then pour off the remaining liquid. Centrifugation can also be used to accelerate the process of phase separation.

Removal of the remaining liquid (solvent) phase requires a drying process, which is typically accompanied by a significant amount of shrinkage and densification. The rate at which the solvent can be removed is ultimately determined by the distribution of porosity in the gel. The ultimate microstructure of the final component will clearly be strongly influenced by changes imposed upon the structural template during this phase of processing. Afterwards, a thermal treatment, or firing process, is often necessary in order to favor further polycondensation and enhance mechanical properties and structural stability via final sintering, densification and grain growth. One of the distinct advantages of using this methodology as opposed to the more traditional processing techniques is that densification is often achieved at a much lower temperature.

The precursor sol can be either deposited on a substrate to form a film (e.g., by dip coating or spin coating), cast into a suitable container with the desired shape (e.g., to obtain monolithic ceramics, glasses, fibres, membranes, aerogels), or used to synthesize powders (e.g., microspheres, nanospheres). The sol-gel approach is a cheap and low-temperature technique that allows for the fine control of the product's chemical composition. Even small quantities of dopants, such as organic dyes and rare earth elements, can be introduced in the sol and end up uniformly dispersed in the final product. It can be used in ceramics processing and manufacturing as an investment casting material, or as a means of producing very thin films of metal oxides for various purposes. Sol-gel derived materials have diverse applications in optics, electronics, energy, space, (bio)sensors, medicine (e.g., controlled drug release), reactive material and separation (e.g., chromatography) technology.

The interest in sol-gel processing can be traced back in the mid-1880s with the observation that the hydrolysis of tetraethyl orthosilicate (TEOS) under acidic conditions led to the formation of SiO_2 in the form of fibres and monoliths.

Sol-gel research grew to be so important that in the 1990s more than 35,000 papers were published worldwide on the process.

Uniformity

In the processing of fine ceramics, the irregular particle sizes and shapes in a typical powder often lead to non-uniform packing morphologies that result in packing density variations in the powder compact. Uncontrolled agglomeration of powders due to attractive van der Waals forces can also give rise to microstructural inhomogeneities.

Differential stresses that develop as a result of non-uniform drying shrinkage are directly related to the rate at which the solvent can be removed, and thus highly dependent upon the distribution of porosity. Such stresses have been associated with a plastic-to-brittle transition in consolidated bodies, and can yield to crack propagation in the unfired body if not relieved.

In addition, any fluctuations in packing density in the compact as it is prepared for the kiln are often amplified during the sintering process, yielding inhomogeneous densification. Some pores and other structural defects associated with density variations have been shown to play a detrimental role in the sintering process by growing and thus limiting end-point densities. Differential stresses arising from inhomogeneous densification have also been shown to result in the propagation of internal cracks, thus becoming the strength-controlling flaws.

It would therefore appear desirable to process a material in such a way that it is physically uniform with regard to the distribution of components and porosity, rather than using particle size distributions which will maximize the green density. The containment of a uniformly dispersed assembly of strongly interacting particles in suspension requires total control over particle-particle interactions. Monodisperse colloids provide this potential.

Electron micrograph of a colloidal crystal composed of amorphous hydrated colloidal silica (particle diameter 600 nm).

Monodisperse powders of colloidal silica, for example, may therefore be stabilized sufficiently to ensure a high degree of order in the colloidal crystal or polycrystalline colloidal solid which results from aggregation. The degree of order appears to be limited by the time and space allowed for longer-range correlations to be established. Such defective polycrystalline colloidal structures would appear to be the basic elements of submicrometre colloidal materials science, and, therefore, provide the first step in developing a more rigorous understanding of the mechanisms involved in microstructural evolution in inorganic systems such as polycrystalline ceramics.

Particles and Polymers

The sol-gel process is a wet-chemical technique used for the fabrication of both glassy and ceramic materials. In this process, the sol (or solution) evolves gradually towards the formation of a gel-like network containing both a liquid phase and a solid phase. Typical precursors are metal alkoxides and metal chlorides, which undergo hydrolysis and polycondensation reactions to form a colloid. The basic structure or morphology of the solid phase can range anywhere from discrete colloidal particles to continuous chain-like polymer networks.

The term *colloid* is used primarily to describe a broad range of solid-liquid (and/or liquid-liquid) mixtures, all of which contain distinct solid (and/or liquid) particles which are dispersed to various degrees in a liquid medium. The term is specific to the size of the individual particles, which are larger than atomic dimensions but small enough to exhibit Brownian motion. If the particles are large enough, then their dynamic behaviour in any given period of time in suspension would be governed by forces of gravity and sedimentation.

But if they are small enough to be colloids, then their irregular motion in suspension can be attributed to the collective bombardment of a myriad of thermally agitated molecules in the liquid suspending medium, as described originally by Albert Einstein in his dissertation. Einstein concluded that this erratic behaviour could adequately be described using the theory of Brownian motion, with sedimentation being a possible long term result. This critical size range (or particle diameter) typically ranges from tens of angstroms (10^{-10} m) to a few micrometres (10^{-6} m).

- Under certain chemical conditions (typically in *base-catalyzed sols*), the particles may grow to sufficient size to become colloids, which are affected both by sedimentation and forces of gravity. Stabilized suspensions of such sub-micrometre spherical particles may eventually result in their self-assembly — yielding highly ordered microstructures reminiscent of the prototype colloidal crystal: precious.
- Under certain chemical conditions (typically in *acid-catalyzed sols*), the interparticle forces have sufficient strength to cause considerable aggregation and/or flocculation prior to their growth. The formation of a more open continuous network of low density polymers exhibits certain advantages with regard to physical properties in the formation of high performance glass and glass/ceramic components in 2 and 3 dimensions.

In either case (discrete particles or continuous polymer network) the sol evolves then towards the formation of an inorganic network containing a liquid phase (gel). Formation of a metal oxide involves connecting the metal centers with oxo (*M-O-M*) or hydroxo (*M-OH-M*) bridges, therefore generating metal-oxo or metal-hydroxo polymers in solution.

In both cases (discrete particles or continuous polymer network), the drying process serves to remove the liquid phase from the gel, yielding a micro-porous amorphous glass or micro-crystalline ceramic. Subsequent thermal treatment (firing) may be performed in order to favour further polycondensation and enhance mechanical properties.

With the viscosity of a sol adjusted into a proper range, both optical quality glass fibre and refractory ceramic fibre can be drawn which are used for fibre optic sensors and thermal insulation, respectively. In addition, uniform ceramic powders of a wide range of chemical composition can be formed by precipitation.

Polymerization

Metal alkoxides are members of the family of organometallic compounds, which are organic compounds which have one or more metal atoms in the molecule. Metal alkoxides (*R-O-M*) are like alcohols (*R-OH*) with a metal atom, M, replacing the hydrogen H in the hydroxyl group. They constitute the class of chemical precursors most widely used in sol-gel synthesis.

The most common mineral in the earth's crust is silicon dioxide (or silica), SiO_2. There are at least seven different crystalline forms of silica, including quartz. The basic building block of all of these crystalline forms of silica is the SiO_4 tetrahedron. Since each tetrahedron shares 2 of its edges with other SiO_4 tetrahedra, the overall ratio of oxygen to silicon is 2:1 instead of 4:1 (thus SiO_2). The intricate and highly specific geometry of this network of tetrahedra takes years to form under incredible terrestrial pressures at great depth. That is why SiO_2 is such a good glass former. Crystallization in a reasonable amount of time under the most ideal laboratory conditions is highly unlikely. Thus, amorphous silica is the major component of nearly all window glass.

A well studied alkoxide is silicon tetraethoxide, or tetraethyl orthosilicate (TEOS). The chemical formula for TEOS is given by: $Si(OC_2H_5)_4$, or $Si(OR)_4$ where the alkyl group $R = C_2H_5$. Alkoxides are ideal chemical precursors for sol-gel synthesis because they react readily with water.

Thus, polymerization is associated with the formation of a 1, 2, or 3- dimensional network of siloxane [*Si–O–Si*] bonds accompanied by the production of *H-O-H* and *R-O-H* species.

By definition, condensation liberates a small molecule, such as water or alcohol. This type of reaction can continue to build larger and larger silicon-containing molecules by the process of polymerization. Thus, a polymer is a huge molecule (or macromolecule) formed from hundreds or thousands of units called monomers. The number of bonds that a monomer can form is called its functionality. Polymerization of silicon alkoxide, for instance, can lead to complex branching of the polymer, because a fully hydrolyzed monomer $Si(OH)_4$ is tetrafunctional (can branch or bond in 4 different directions). Alternatively, under certain conditions (e.g., low water concentration) fewer than 4 of the OR or OH groups (ligands) will be capable of condensation, so relatively little branching will occur. The mechanisms of hydrolysis and condensation, and the factors that bias the structure toward linear or branched structures are the most critical issues of sol-gel science and technology.

Applications

The applications for sol gel-derived products are numerous. For example, scientists have used it to produce the world's lightest materials and also some of its toughest ceramics. One of the largest application areas is thin films, which can be produced on a piece of substrate by spin coating or dip coating. Other methods include spraying, electrophoresis, inkjet printing or roll coating. Optical coatings, protective and decorative coatings, and electro-optic components can be applied to glass, metal and other types of substrates with these methods.

Cast into a mold, and with further drying and heat-treatment, dense ceramic or glass articles with novel properties can be formed that cannot be created by any other method. Macroscopic optical elements and active optical components as well as large area hot mirrors, cold mirrors, lenses and beam splitters all with optimal geometry can be made quickly and at low cost via the sol-gel route.

With the viscosity of a sol adjusted into a proper range, both optical and refractory ceramic fibres can be drawn which are used for fibre optic sensors and thermal insulation, respectively.

Ultra-fine and uniform ceramic powders can be formed by precipitation. These powders of single and multiple component compositions can be made in sub-micrometre particle size for dental and biomedical applications. Composite powders have been patented for use as agrochemicals and herbicides. Powder abrasives, used in a variety of finishing operations, are made using a sol-gel type process.

One of the more important applications of sol-gel processing is to carry out zeolite synthesis. Other elements (metals, metal oxides) can be easily incorporated into the final product and the silicate sol formed by this method is very stable.

Another application in research is to entrap biomolecules for sensory (biosensors) or catalytic purposes, by physically or chemically preventing them from leaching out and, in the case of protein or chemically-linked small molecules, by shielding them from the external environment yet allowing small molecules to be monitored. The major disadvantages are that the change in local environment may alter the functionality of the protein or small molecule entrapped and that the synthesis step may damage the protein. To circumvent this, various strategies have been explored, such as monomers with protein friendly leaving groups (e.g. glycerol) and the inclusion of polymers which stabilize protein.

Other products fabricated with this process include various ceramic membranes for microfiltration, ultrafiltration, nanofiltration, pervaporation and reverse osmosis.

If the liquid in a wet gel is removed under a supercritical condition, a highly porous and extremely low density material called aerogel is obtained. Drying the gel by means of low temperature treatments (25-100°C), it is possible to obtain porous solid matrices called xerogels.

Finally of historical note, a sol-gel process was developed in the 1950s for the production of radioactive powders of UO_2 and ThO_2 for nuclear fuels, without generation of large quantities of dust.

6

Glass Production

Glass production comprehends two types of glass:

(i) sheet glass, made by the float glass process; and

(ii) glass-container glass.

Glass Container Factories

Broadly, modern glass container factories are three-part operations: the *batch house*, the *hot end*, and the *cold end*. The *batch house* handles the raw materials; the *hot end* handles the manufacture proper — the furnaces, annealing ovens, and forming machines; and the *cold end* handles the product-inspection and -packaging equipment.

Furnace

The *hot end* of a glassworks is where the molten glass is formed into containers; beginning when the batch is fed into the furnace at a slow, controlled rate. The furnaces are natural gas- or fuel oil-fired, and operate at temperatures up to 1675°C. The temperature is limited only by the quality of the furnace's superstructure material and by the glass composition.

Forming Process

There are, currently, two primary methods of making a glass container — the *blow and blow* method and the *press and blow* method. In both cases a stream of molten glass, at its plastic temperature (1050°C-1200°C), is cut with a shearing blade to form a cylinder of glass, called a *gob*. Both processes start with the *gob* falling, by gravity, and guided, through troughs and chutes, into the blank moulds. In the blow and blow process, the glass is first blown from below, into the blank moulds, to create a *parison*, or pre-container. The *parison* is then flipped over into a final mould, where a *final blow* blows the glass out, in to the mould, to make the final container shape. In the case of *press and blow* process, the *parison* is formed with a metal plunger, which pushes the glass out, into the blank mould. The process then continues as before, with the *parison* being transferred to the mould, and the glass being blown out into the mould.

The forming machines hold and move the parts that form the container. Generally powered by compressed air, the mechanisms are timed to coordinate the movement of all these parts so that containers are made.

The most widely used forming machine arrangement is the *individual section* machine (or IS machine). This machine has a bank of 5-20 identical sections, each of which contains one complete set of mechanisms to make containers. The sections are in a row, and the gobs feed into each section via a moving chute, called the *gob distributor*. Sections make either one, two, three or four containers simultaneously. (Referred to as *single*, *double*, *triple* and *quad* gob). In the case of multiple gobs, the *shears* cut the *gobs* simultaneously, and they fall into the blank moulds in parallel.

Internal Treatment

After the forming process, some containers — particularly those intended for alcoholic spirits — undergo a treatment to improve the chemical resistance of the inside, called *internal treatment* or dealkalization. This is usually accomplished through the injection of a sulfur- or fluorine-containing gas mixture into bottles at high temperatures.

The gas is typically delivered to the container either in the air used in the forming process (that is, during the final blow of the container), or through a nozzle directing a stream of the gas into the mouth of the bottle after forming. The treatment renders the container more resistant to alkali extraction, which can cause increases in product pH, and in some cases container degradation.

Annealing

As glass cools it shrinks and solidifies. Uneven cooling causes weak glass due to stress. Even cooling is achieved by annealing. An annealing oven (known in the industry as a Lehr) heats the container to about 580°C then cools it, depending on the glass thickness, over a 20-6000 minute period.

Inspection Equipment

Glass containers are 100 per cent inspected; automatic machines, or sometimes persons, inspect every container for a variety of faults. Typical faults include small cracks in the glass called *checks* and foreign inclusions called *stones* which are pieces of the refractory brick lining of the melting furnace that break off and fall into the pool of molten glass which subsequently are included in the final product. These are especially important to select out due to the fact that they can impart a destructive element to the final glass product. For example, since these materials can withstand large amounts of themal energy, they can cause the glass product to sustain thermal shock resulting in explosive destruction when heated. Other defects include bubbles in the glass called *blisters* and excessively thin walls. Another defect common in glass manufacturing is referred to as a *tear*. In the *press and blow* forming, if a plunger and mould are out of alignment, or heated to an incorrect temperature, the glass will stick to either item and become torn. In addition to rejecting faulty containers, inspection equipment gathers statistical information and relays it to the forming machine operators in the hot end. Computer systems collect fault information to the mould that produced the container. This is done by reading the mould number on the container, which is encoded (as a numeral, or a binary code of dots) on the container by the mould that made it. Operators carry out a range of checks manually on samples of containers, usually visual and dimensional checks.

Secondary Processing

Sometimes container factories will offer services such as labelling. Several labelling technologies are available. Unique to glass is the *Applied Ceramic Labelling* process (ACL). This is screen-printing of the decoration onto the container with a vitreous enamel paint, which is then baked on. An example of this is the original Coca-Cola bottle. The Absolut Bottles have various added services such as: Etching (Absolut Citron/) Coating (Absolut Raspberry/Ruby Red)and *Applied Ceramic Labelling* (Absolut Blue/Pears/Red/Black).

Packaging

Glass containers are packaged in various ways. Popular in Europe are bulk pallets with between 1000 and 4000 containers each. This is carried out by automatic machines (palletisers) which arrange and stack containers separated by layer sheets. Other possibilities include boxes and even hand sewn sacks. Once packed the new 'stock units' are labelled and warehoused.

Cold End

The role of the *cold end* is to inspect the containers for defects, package the containers for shipment and label the containers.

Coatings

Glass containers typically receive two surface coatings, one at the *hot end*, just before annealing and one at the *cold end* just after annealing. At the *hot end* a very thin layer of tin oxide is applied either using a safe organic compound or inorganic stannic chloride. Tin based systems are not the only ones used, although the most popular. Titanium tetrachloride or organo titanates can also be used. In all cases the coating renders the surface of the glass more adhesive to the *cold end* coating. At the *cold end* a layer of typically, polyethylene wax, is applied via a water based emulsion. This makes the glass slippery, protecting it from scratching and stopping containers from sticking together when they are moved on a conveyor. The resultant invisible combined coating gives a virtually unscratchable surface to the glass. Due to reduction of in-service surface damage the coatings often are described as strengtheners, however a more correct definition might be strength retaining coatings.

Ancillary Processes — Compressors and Cooling

Forming machines are largely powered by compressed air and a typical glass works will have several large compressors (totaling 30k-60k cfm) to provide the needed compressed air. Furnaces, compressors and forming machine generate quantities of waste heat which is generally cooled by water. Hot glass which is not used in the forming machine is diverted and this diverted glass (called *cullet*) is generally cooled by water, and sometime even processed and crushed in a water bath arrangement. Often cooling requirements are shared over banks of cooling towers arranged to allow for backup during maintenance.

Marketing

Glass container manufacture in the developed world is a mature market business. Annual growth in total industry sales generally follows population growth. Glass container manufacture is also a geographical business; the product is heavy and large in volume, and the major raw materials (sand, soda ash and limestone) are generally readily available, therefore production facilities need to be located close to their markets. A typical glass furnace holds hundreds of tonnes of molten glass, and so it is simply not practical to shut it down every night, or in fact in any period short of a month. Factories therefore run 24 hours a day 7 days a week. This means that there is little opportunity to either increase or decrease production rates by more than a few per cent. New furnaces and forming machines cost tens of millions of dollars and require at least 18 months of planning. Given this fact, and the fact that there are usually more products than machine lines means that products are sold from stock. The marketing/production challenge is therefore to be able to predict demand both in the short 4-12 week term and over the 24-48 month long term. Factories are generally sized to service the requirements of a city; in developed countries there is usually a factory per 1-2 million people. A typical factory will produce 1-3 million containers a day. Despite its positioning as a mature market product, glass does enjoy a high level of consumer acceptance and is perceived as a 'premium' quality packaging format.

Lifecycle Impact

Glass containers are wholly recyclable and the industry in many countries retains a policy (or is forced to by Government) of maintaining a high price on cullet to ensure high return rates. Return rates of 95 per cent are not uncommon in the Nordic countries (Sweden, Norway, Denmark and Finland). Return rates of less than 50 per cent are usual in other countries. Of course glass containers can also be reused, and in developing countries this is common, however the environmental impact of washing the container as against remelting them is uncertain. Factors to consider here are the chemicals and fresh water used in the washing, and the fact that a single use container can be made much lighter, using less than half the glass (and therefore energy content) of a multiuse container. Also, a significant factor in the developed world's consideration of reuse are producer concerns over the risk and consequential product liability of using a component (the reused container) of unknown and unqualified safety. How glass containers compare to other packaging types (plastic, cardboard, aluminium) is hard to say, conclusive lifecycle studies are yet to be produced.

Local Environmental Impacts

As with all highly concentrated industries, glassworks suffer from moderately high local environmental impacts. Compounding this is that because they are mature market businesses they often have been located on the same site for a long time and this has resulted in residential encroachment. The main impacts on residential housing and cities are noise, fresh water use, water pollution, NOx and SOx air pollution, and dust.

Noise is created by the forming machines. Operated by compressed air, they can produce noise levels of up to 106dBA. How this noise is carried into the local neighbourhood depends heavily on the layout of the factory. Another factor in noise production is truck movements. A typical factory will process 600T of material a day. This means that some 600T of raw material has to come onto the site and the same off the site again as finished product.

Water is used to cool the furnace, compressor and unused molten glass. Water use in factories varies widely, it can be as little as one tonne water used per melted tonne of glass. Of the one tonne roughly half is evaporated to provide cooling, the rest forms a wastewater stream.

Most factories use water containing an emulsified oil to cool and lubricate the *gob* cutting *shear blades*. This oil laden water mixes with the water outflow stream thus polluting it. Factories usually have some kind water processing equipment that removes this emulsified oil to various degrees of effectiveness.

The oxides of nitrogen are a natural product of the burning of gas in air and are produced in large quantities by gas fired furnaces. Some factories in cities with particular air pollution problems will mitigate this by using liquid oxygen, however the logic of this given the cost in carbon of:

1. not using regenerators; and
2. having to liquefy and transport oxygen is highly questionable.

The oxides of sulphur are produced as a result of the glass melting process. Manipulating the batch formula can effect some limited mitigation of this; alternatively exhaust plume scrubbing can be used.

The raw materials for glass making are all dusty material and are delivered either as a powder or as a fine-grained material. Systems for controlling dusty materials tend to be difficult to maintain, and given the large amounts of material moved each day, only a small amount has to escape for there to be a dust problem. *Cullet* is also moved about in a glass factory and tends to produce fine glass particles when shovelled or broken.

Global Environmental Impact

The main global impact factor is the production of CO_2 due to the burning of fossil fuels in the heating of the furnace and production of electricity to supply the compressors. Typically a tonne of glass packed will liberate between 500 and 900 kg of CO_2, assuming a gas fired furnace and coal fired electricity usage. In areas with predominantly renewable or nuclear energy, the CO_2 released comes only from the conversion of carbonates to oxides in the ingredients of the glass itself.

Float Glass

Float glass is a sheet of glass made by floating molten glass on a bed of molten metal, typically tin, although lead and various low melting point alloys were used in the past. This method gives the sheet uniform thickness and very flat surfaces. Modern windows are made from float glass. Most float glass is soda-lime glass, but relatively minor quantities of specialty borosilicate and flat panel display glass are also produced using the float glass process. The float glass process is also known as the Pilkington process, named after the British glass manufacturer Pilkington, which pioneered the technique (invented by Sir Alastair Pilkington) in the 1950s.

Until the 17th century, window glass or flat glass was generally cut from large discs (or rondels) of crown glass. Larger sheets of glass were made by blowing large cylinders which were cut open and flattened, then cut into panes. Most window glass in the early 19th century was made using the cylinder method. The 'cylinders' were 6 to 8 feet (1.8 to 2.4 m) long and 10 to 14 inches (250 to 360 mm) in diameter, limiting the width that panes of glass could be cut, and resulting in windows divided by transoms into rectangular panels.

The first advances in automating glass manufacturing were patented in 1848 by Henry Bessemer, an English engineer. His system produced a continuous ribbon of flat glass by forming the ribbon between rollers. This was an expensive process, as the surfaces of the glass needed polishing. If the glass could be set on a perfectly smooth body this would cut costs considerably. Attempts were made to form flat glass on a molten tin bath, notably in the US. Several patents were awarded, but this process was unworkable.

Before the development of float glass, larger sheets of plate glass were made by casting a large puddle of glass on an iron surface, and then polishing both sides, a costly process. From the early 1920s, a continuous ribbon of plate glass was passed through a lengthy series of inline grinders and polishers, reducing glass losses and cost.

Glass of lower quality, sheet glass, was made by drawing upwards from a pool of molten glass a thin sheet, held at the edges by rollers. As it cooled the rising sheet stiffened and could then be cut. The two surfaces were not as smooth or uniform, and of lower quality than those of float glass. This process continued in use for many years after the development of float glass.

Between 1953 and 1957, Sir Alastair Pilkington and Kenneth Bickerstaff of the UK's Pilkington Brothers developed the first successful commercial application for forming a continuous ribbon of glass using a molten tin bath on which the molten glass flows unhindered under the influence of gravity. The success of this process lay in the careful balance of the volume of glass fed onto the bath, where it was flattened by its own weight. Full scale profitable sales of float glass were first achieved in 1960.

Manufacture

Float glass uses common glass making raw materials, typically consisting of sand, soda ash (sodium carbonate), dolomite, limestone, and salt cake (sodium sulfate). Other materials may be used as colourants, refining agents or to adjust the physical and chemical properties of the glass. The raw materials are mixed in a batch mixing process, then fed together with suitable cullet (waste glass), in a controlled ratio, into a furnace where it is heated to approximately 1500°C. Common flat glass furnaces are 9 m wide, 45 m long, and contain more than 1200 tons of glass. Once molten, the temperature of the glass is stabilised to approximately 1200°C to ensure a homogeneous specific gravity.

The molten glass is fed into a 'tin bath', a bath of molten tin (about 3-4 m wide, 50 m long, 6 cm deep), from a delivery canal and is poured into the tin bath by a ceramic lip known as the spout lip. The amount of glass allowed to pour onto the molten tin is controlled by a gate known as a Tweel.

Tin is suitable for the float glass process because it has a high specific gravity, is cohesive, and immiscible into the molten glass. Tin, however, is highly reactive with oxygen and oxidises in a natural atmosphere to form Tin dioxide

(SnO_2). Known in the production process as dross, the tin dioxide adheres to the glass. To prevent oxidation, the tin bath is provided with a positive pressure protective atmosphere consisting of a mixture of nitrogen and hydrogen.

The glass flows onto the tin surface forming a floating ribbon with perfectly smooth surfaces on both sides and an even thickness. As the glass flows along the tin bath, the temperature is gradually reduced from 1100°C until the sheet can be lifted from the tin onto rollers at approximately 600°C. The glass ribbon is pulled off the bath by rollers at a controlled speed. Variation in the flow speed and roller speed enables glass sheets of varying thickness to be formed. Top rollers positioned above the molten tin may be used to control both the thickness and the width of the glass ribbon.

Once off the bath, the glass sheet passes through a lehr kiln for approximately 100 m, where it is further cooled gradually so that it anneals without strain and does not crack from the change in temperature. On exiting the 'cold end' of the kiln, the glass is cut by machines.

Borosilicate Glass

Borosilicate glass is a type of glass with the main glass-forming constituents silica and boron oxide. Borosilicate glasses are known for having very low coefficients of thermal expansion ($\sim 5 \times 10^{-6}$/°C at 20°C), making them resistant to thermal shock, more so than any other common glass.

Borosilicate glass was first developed by German glassmaker Otto Schott in the late 19th century and sold under the brand name 'Duran' in 1893. After Corning Glass Works introduced Pyrex in 1915, it became a synonym for borosilicate glass in the English-speaking world.

The European manufacturer of Pyrex, Arc International, uses borosilicate glass in its Pyrex glass kitchen products; however, the U.S. manufacturer of Pyrex kitchenware uses tempered soda-lime glass. Thus Pyrex can refer to either soda-lime glass or borosilicate glass when discussing kitchen glassware, while Pyrex, Bomex, Duran and Kimax all refer to borosilicate glass when discussing laboratory glassware.

Most borosilicate glass is colorless. Colored borosilicate, for the studio glass trade, was first widely brought onto the market in 1986 when Paul Trautman founded Northstar Glassworks. There are now a number of small companies in the U.S. and abroad that manufacture and sell colored borosilicate glass for use in studio glass.

In addition to the quartz, sodium carbonate, and calcium carbonate traditionally used in glassmaking, boron is used in the manufacture of borosilicate glass. Typically, the resulting glass composition is about 70 per cent silica, 10 per cent boron oxide, 8 per cent sodium oxide, 8 per cent potassium oxide, and 1 per cent calcium oxide (lime). Though somewhat more difficult to make than traditional glass (Corning conducted a major revamp of their operations to make it), it is economical to produce; its superior durability, chemical and heat resistance finds excellent use in chemical laboratory equipment, cookware, lighting and, in certain cases, windows.

Manufacturing Process

Borosilicate glass is created by adding boron to the traditional glassmaker's frit of silicate sand, soda, and ground lime. Since borosilicate glass melts at a higher temperature than ordinary silicate glass, some new techniques were required for industrial production. Borrowing from the welding trade, burners combining oxygen with natural gas were required.

Composition and Physical Characteristics

Borosilicate glass has a very low thermal expansion coefficient, about one-third that of ordinary glass. This reduces material stresses caused by temperature gradients, thus making it more resistant to breaking. This makes it a popular material for objects like telescope mirrors, where it is essential to have very little deviation in shape. It is also used in the processing of high-level radioactive waste, where the waste is immobilised in the glass through a process known as vitrification (contrast with Synroc).

The softening point (temperature at which viscosity is approximately $10^{7.6}$ poise) of type 7740 Pyrex is 820°C (1,510°F).

While more resistant to thermal shock than other types of glass, borosilicate glass can still crack or shatter when subject to rapid or uneven temperature variations. When broken, borosilicate glass tends to crack into large pieces rather than shattering (it will snap rather than splinter).

Optically, borosilicate glasses are crown glasses with low dispersion (Abbe numbers around 65) and relatively low refractive indices (1.51-1.54 across the visible range).

The refractory properties and physical strength of borosilicate glass make it ideal for use in high-durability laboratory equipment such as beakers and test tubes. In addition, borosilicate glass warps minimally when exposed to heat, allowing a borosilicate container to provide accurate measurements of volume over time.

During the mid-twentieth century, borosilicate glass tubing was used to pipe coolants (often distilled water) through high power vacuum tube-based electronic equipment, such as commercial broadcast transmitters.

Glass cookware is another common usage. Borosilicate glass measuring cups, featuring screen printed markings providing graduated measurements, are widely used in American kitchens.

Aquarium heaters are sometimes made of borosilicate glass. Due to its high heat resistance, it can tolerate the significant temperature difference between the water and the nichrome heating element.

Many high-quality flashlights use borosilicate glass for the lens. This allows for a higher percentage of light transmittance through the lens compared to plastics and lower-quality glass.

Specialty marijuana and tobacco pipes are made from borosilicate glass. The high heat resistance makes the pipes more durable.

Most premanufactured glass guitar slides are also made of borosilicate glass.

New lampworking techniques led to artistic applications such as contemporary glass marbles. The modern studio glass movement, spurred largely by the rapid development of a borosilicate colour palette at Northstar Glass in the 1980s and 1990s, has provided good economic growth for borosilicate glass suppliers. Borosilicate is commonly used in the glassblowing form of lampworking and the artists create a range of products ranging from jewellery, kitchenware, to sculpture as well as for artistic glass tobacco pipes.

Borosilicate glass is sometimes used for high-quality beverage glassware. Borosilicate glass lends kitchen-and glassware increased durability along with microwave and dishwasher compatibility.

Most astronomical reflecting telescope glass mirror components are made of borosilicate glass because of its low coefficient of expansion with heat. This makes very precise optical surfaces possible that change very little with temperature, and matched glass mirror components that 'track' across temperature changes and retain the optical system's characteristics.

The optical glass most often used for making instrument lenses is Schott BK-7 (or the equivalent from other makers), a very finely made borosilicate crown glass. It is also designated as 517642 glass after its 1.517 refractive index and 64.2 Abbe number. Other less costly borosilicate glasses, such as Schott B270 or the equivalent, are used to make 'crown glass' eyeglass lenses. Ordinary lower-cost borosilicate glass, like that used to make kitchenware and even reflecting telescope mirrors, cannot be used for high-quality lenses because of the striations and inclusions common to lower grades of this type of glass.

Borosilicate is also a material of choice for evacuated tube solar thermal technology, because of its high strength and heat resistance.

Borosilicate glasses also find application in the semiconductor industry in the development of microelectromechanical systems (MEMS), as part of stacks of etched silica wafers bonded to the etched borosilicate glass.

The thermal insulation tiles on the Space Shuttle are coated with a borosilicate glass.

Lighting manufacturers use borosilicate glass in their refractors.

Additionally, borosilicate tubing is used as the feedstock for the production of parenteral drug packaging, such as vials and pre-filled syringes, and is also used for the production of ampoules and dental cartridges. The chemical resistance of borosilicate glass minimizes the migration of sodium ions from the glass matrix thus making it well suited for injectable drug applications. This type of glass is typically referred to as USP/EP JP Type I.

Borosilicate glasses are used for immobilisation and disposal of radioactive wastes. In most countries high-level radioactive waste has been incorporated into alkali borosilicate or phosphate vitreous waste forms for many years and vitrification is an established technology. Vitrification is a particularly attractive immobilization route because of the high chemical durability of the vitrified glass product. This characteristic has been used by industry for centuries. The chemical resistance of glass can allow it to remain in a corrosive environment for many thousands and even millions of years.

Borosilicate Nanoparticles

It was initially thought that borosilicate glass could not be formed into nanoparticles, since an unstable boron oxide precursor prevented successful forming of these shapes. However, in 2008 a team of researchers from the Swiss Federal Institute of Technology at Lausanne were successful in forming borosilicate nanoparticles of 100 to 500 nanometers in diameter. The researchers formed a gel of tetraethylorthosilicate and trimethoxyboroxine. When this gel is exposed to water under proper conditions, a dynamic reaction ensues which results in the nanoparticles.

In Lampworking

Borosilicate, or 'boro' as it is often referred to, is used extensively in the glassblowing process lampworking, which involves using a burner torch to melt and form glass, using a variety of metal and graphite tools. Borosilicate is referred to as 'hard glass' and has a higher melting point than 'soft glass' which is used in glassblowing formed in large furnaces and large rods. Raw glass used in lampworking comes in glass rods for solid work and glass tubes for hollow work tubes and vessels/containers. Lampworking is used to make complex and custom scientific apparatus; most major universities have a lampworking shop to manufacture and repair their glassware. For this kind of 'scientific glassblowing', the specifications must be exact and the glassblower must be highly skilled and precise. Lampworking is also done as art and common items made include goblets, paper weights and pendants. Borosilicate often has a more three dimensional and exotic look than soft glass, with natural and multicoloured tones to it. Colours in glass come from combining different amounts of elements, including cobalt, iron, and silver.

7

Optical Lens Design

Optical lens design refers to the calculation of lens construction parameters (variables) that will meet a set of performance requirements and constraints, including cost and schedule limitations.

Construction parameters include surface profile types (spherical, aspheric, holographic, diffractive, etc.), and the parameters for each surface type such as radius of curvature, distance to the next surface, glass type and optionally tilt and decenter.

Design Requirements

Performance requirements can include:

- Optical performance, i.e., image quality: quantified by encircled energy, modulation transfer function, Strehl ratio, ghost reflection control, and pupil performance (size, location and aberration control); the choice of the image quality metric is application specific.
- Physical requirements such as weight, static volume, dynamic volume, center of gravity and overall configuration requirements.
- Environmental requirements: ranges for temperature, pressure, vibration and electromagnetic shielding.

Design constraints can include realistic lens element center and edge thicknesses, minimum and maximum air-spaces between lenses, maximum constraints on entrance and exit angles, physically realizable glass index of refraction and dispersion properties.

Manufacturing costs and delivery schedules are also a major part of optical design. The price of an optical glass blank of given dimensions can vary by a factor of fifty or more, depending on the size, glass type, index homogeneity quality, and availability, with BK7 usually being the cheapest. Costs for larger and/or thicker optical blanks of a given material, above 100mm to 150mm or so, usually increase faster than what would be proportional to just the increase in physical volume. This is primarily due to increased blank annealing time required to achieve acceptable index homogeneity and internal stress birefringence levels throughout the blank volume. Availability of glass blanks is driven by how frequently a particular glass type is mixed and poured by a given manufacturer, and can seriously affect manufacturing cost and schedule.

Process

Lenses can first be designed using paraxial theory to position images and pupils, then real surfaces inserted and optimized. Paraxial theory can be skipped in simpler cases and the lens directly optimized using real surfaces. Lenses are first designed using average index of refraction and dispersion (see Abbe number) properties published in the glass manufacturer's catalog and though glass model calculations. However, the properties of the real glass blanks will vary from this ideal; index of refraction values can vary by as much as 0.0003 or more from catalog values, and dispersion can either remain about the same or vary slightly. These changes in index and dispersion can sometimes be enough to affect the lens focus location and imaging performance in highly corrected systems.

The lens blank manufacturing process is as follows:

- the glass batch ingredients for a desired glass type are mixed together in a powder state;
- the powder mixture is melted together in a furnace;
- the fluid is further mixed while molten to maximize batch homogeneity;
- poured into lens blanks; and
- annealed according to empirically determined time-temperature schedules.

The glass blank pedigree, or 'melt data', can be determined for a given glass batch by making small precision prisms from various locations in the batch and measuring their index of refraction on a spectrometer, typically at five or more wavelengths. Lens design programmes have curve fitting routines that can fit the melt data to a selected dispersion curve, from which the index of refraction at any wavelength within the fitted wavelength range can be calculated. A re-optimization, or 'melt re-comp', can then be performed on the lens design using measured index of refraction data where available. When manufactured, the resulting lens performance will more closely match the desired requirements than if average glass catalog values for index of refraction were assumed.

Delivery schedules are impacted by glass and mirror blank availability and lead times to acquire, the amount of tooling a shop must fabricate prior to starting on a project, the manufacturing tolerances on the parts (tighter tolerances mean longer fab times), the complexity of any optical coatings that must be applied to the finished parts, further complexities in mounting or bonding lens elements into cells and in the overall lens system assembly, and any post-assembly alignment and quality control testing and tooling required. Tooling costs and delivery schedules can be reduced by using existing tooling at any given shop wherever possible, and by maximizing manufacturing tolerances to the extent possible.

Lens Optimization

Optical design is partly a science because ray paths and wavefront structure can be very accurately calculated anywhere along the propagation path through the lens. Glass and coating optical properties can be measured and modelled with sufficient precision for use in lenses. If tolerances are included during the design, parts can usually be manufactured accurately enough that the resulting lens assembly performs acceptably close to the paper design.

Optical design is also partly an art, though, as the multi-dimensional design space within which a constrained lens design is free to roam is literally beyond human imagination if more than a few construction parameters are free to vary. The number, type and placement of optical elements are partly driven by physical requirements, but are also often based on previous similar designs obtained from published data, patents and textbooks. Skill and intuition in lens design are acquired over years of experience spanning hundreds to thousands of different lens design projects, preferably leading to additional experiences (and headaches) dealing with fabricating and aligning systems.

As an example of the complexity of lens-design space, a simple two-element air-spaced lens has nine variables (four radii of curvature, two thicknesses, one airspace thickness, and two glass types). Even for this simplest case, the design space is thus nine-dimensional, and local or global solutions within this space can at least be imagined as smaller or larger bubbles in a sponge-like 9-D foam-scape. A complex multi-configuration lens corrected over a wide spectral band and field of view, at multiple zoomed focal lengths and over a realistic temperature range, can have an extremely complex design volume, having over a hundred dimensions.

Lens optimization techniques that can navigate this multi-dimensional space and proceed to local minima have been studied since the 1940s, beginning with early work by James G. Baker, and later by D. Feder, Wynne, Glatzel, D. Grey and others. Prior to the advent of digital computers, lens design was an agonizingly slow hand-calculation process requiring high-precision trigonometric and logarithmic tables, reams of paper, plotting 2-D cuts through the multi-dimensional space, and significant patience and understudying from previous masters. Tracing a single ray through a given lens surface could take more than an hour of painstaking calculations and checks, and a lens designer could not design more than a very few complex, high-performance anastigmatic objectives in an entire lifetime.

Modern desktop computers can now raytrace tens to hundreds of millions of rays per second through a lens, and perform hundreds to thousands of optimization cycles per second, rapidly exploring the n-dimensional design volume and even hill-climbing in and out of local minima in the search for the best solution.

However, even with lightning-fast optimizers, seasoned experience is still needed to guide solution trajectories through unacceptably shallow local minima and achieve the desired performance requirements. Experience in the mechanical and physical properties of glass, metals, optical coatings and bonding materials is also needed, especially in systems required to give high sustained performance over wide temperature ranges and harsh environmental conditions.

8

Glass Colouring

Glass colouring and *colour marking* may be obtained by:

1. addition of *colouring ions*
2. precipitation of nanometer sized colloides (so-called *striking glasses* such as 'ruby gold' or red 'selenium ruby';
3. *coloured inclusions* (as in milk glass and smoked glass);
4. *light scattering* (as in phase separated glass);
5. *dichroic coatings* (see dichroic glass); and
6. *coloured coatings.*

Ordinary soda-lime glass appears colourless to the naked eye when it is thin, although iron oxide impurities produce a green tint which can be viewed in thick pieces or with the aid of scientific instruments. Further metals and metal oxides can be added to glass during its manufacture to change its colour which can enhance its aesthetic appeal.

Iron(II) oxide may be added to glass resulting in bluish-green glass which is frequently used in beer bottles. Together withchromium it gives a richer green colour, used for wine bottles.

Sulphur, together with carbon and iron salts, is used to form iron polysulphides and produce amber glass ranging from yellowish to almost black. In borosilicate glasses rich in boron, sulphur imparts a blue colour. With calcium it yields a deep yellow colour.

Manganese can be added in small amounts to remove the green tint given by iron, or in higher concentrations to give glass an amethyst colour. Manganese is one of the oldest glass additives, and purple manganese glass was used since early Egyptian history.

Manganese dioxide, which is black, is used to remove the green colour from the glass; in a very slow process this is converted to sodium permanganate, a dark purple compound. In New England some houses built more than 300 years ago have window glass which is lightly tinted violet because of this chemical change; and such glass panes are prized as antiques.

Small concentrations of cobalt (0.025 to 0.1%) yield blue glass. The best results are achieved when using glass containing potash. Very small amounts can be used for decolourizing.

2 to 3 per cent of copper oxide produces a turquoise colour. Nickel, depending on the concentration, produces blue, or violet, or even black glass. Lead crystal with added nickel acquires purplish colour. Nickel together with a small amount of cobalt was used for decolourizing of lead glass. Chromium is a very powerful colourizing agent, yielding dark green or in higher concentrations even black colour. Together with tin oxide and arsenic it yields emerald green glass. Chromium aventurine, in which aventurescence was achieved by growth of large parallel chromium(III) oxide plates, was also made from glass with added chromium. Cadmium together with sulphur results in deep yellow colour, often used in glazes. However, cadmium is toxic. Adding titanium produces yellowish-brown glass. Titanium, rarely used on its own, is more often employed to intensify and brighten other colourizing additives. Uranium (0.1 to 2%) can be added to give glass a fluorescent yellow or green colour. Uranium glass is typically not radioactive enough to be dangerous, but if ground into a powder, such as by polishing with sandpaper, and inhaled, it can be carcinogenic. When

used with lead glass with very high proportion of lead, produces a deep red colour.

Selenium, like manganese, can be used in small concentrations to decolourize glass, or in higher concentrations to impart a reddish colour, caused by selenium nanoparticles dispersed in glass. It is a very important agent to make pink and red glass. When used together with cadmium sulfide, it yields a brilliant red colour known as 'Selenium Ruby'.

Pure metallic copper produces a very dark red, opaque glass, which is sometimes used as a substitute for gold in the production of ruby-coloured glass. Metallic gold, in very small concentrations (around 0.001%), produces a rich ruby-coloured glass ('Ruby Gold'), while lower concentrations produces a less intense red, often marketed as 'cranberry'. The colour is caused by the size and dispersion of gold particles. Ruby gold glass is usually made of lead glass with added tin. Silver compounds such as silver nitrate and silver halides can produce a range of colours from orange-red to yellow. The way the glass is heated and cooled can significantly affect the colours produced by these compounds. Also photochromic lenses and photosensitive glass are based on silver.

Glass containing two or more phases with different refractive indices shows colouring based on the Tyndall effect and explained by the Mie theory, if the dimensions of the phases are similar or larger than the wavelength of visible light. The scattered light is blue and violet as seen in the image, while the transmitted light is yellow and red.

Dichroic Glass

Dichroic glass has one or several coatings in the nanometer-range (for example metals, metal oxides, or nitrides) which give the glass dichroic optical properties. Also the blue appearance of some automobile windshields is caused by dichroism.

9

History of Optics

Optics began with the development of lenses by the ancient Egyptians and Mesopotamians, followed by theories on light and vision developed by ancient Greek and Indian philosophers, and the development of geometrical optics in the Greco-Roman world. The word *optics* is derived from the Greek term which refers to matters of vision. Optics was significantly reformed by the developments in the mediaeval Islamic world, such as the beginnings of physical and physiological optics, and then significantly advanced in early modern Europe, where diffractive optics began. These earlier studies on optics are now known as 'classical optics'. The term 'modern optics' refers to areas of optical research that largely developed in the 20th century, such as wave optics and quantum optics.

Early History of Optics

The earliest known lenses were made from polished crystal, often quartz, and have been dated as early as 700 BC for Assyrian lenses such as the Layard/Nimrud lens. There are many similar lenses from ancient Egypt, Greece and Babylon. The ancient Romans and Greeks filled glass spheres with water to make lenses. However, glass lenses were not thought of until the Middle Ages.

Some lenses fixed in ancient Egyptian statues are much older than those mentioned above. There is some doubt as to whether or not they qualify as lenses, but they are undoubtedly glass and served at least ornamental purposes. The statues appear to be anatomically correct schematic eyes.

In ancient India, the philosophical schools of Samkhya and Vaisheshika, from around the 6th-5th century BC, developed theories on light. According to the Samkhya school, light is one of the five fundamental 'subtle' elements (*tanmatra*) out of which emerge the gross elements.

In contrast, the Vaisheshika school gives an atomic theory of the physical world on the non-atomic ground of ether, space and time. The basic atoms are those of earth (*prthivi*), water (*apas*), fire (*tejas*), and air (*vayu*), that should not be confused with the ordinary meaning of these terms. These atoms are taken to form binary molecules that combine further to form larger molecules. Motion is defined in terms of the movement of the physical atoms. Light rays are taken to be a stream of high velocity of *tejas* (fire) atoms. The particles of light can exhibit different characteristics depending on the speed and the arrangements of the *tejas* atoms. Around the first century BC, the *Vishnu Purana* refers to sunlight as the 'the seven rays of the sun'.

In the fifth century BC, Empedocles postulated that everything was composed of four elements; fire, air, earth and water. He believed that Aphrodite made the human eye out of the four elements and that she lit the fire in the eye which shone out from the eye making sight possible. If this were true, then one could see during the night just as well as during the day, so Empedocles postulated an interaction between rays from the eyes and rays from a source such as the sun.

In his *Optics* Greek mathematician Euclid observed that "things seen under a greater angle appear greater, and those under a lesser angle less, while those under equal angles appear equal". In the 36 propositions that follow,

Euclid relates the apparent size of an object to its distance from the eye and investigates the apparent shapes of cylinders and cones when viewed from different angles. Pappus believed these results to be important in astronomy and included Euclid's *Optics*, along with his *Phaenomena*, in the *Little Astronomy*, a compendium of smaller works to be studied before the *Syntaxis* (*Almagest*) of Ptolemy.

In 55 BC, Lucretius, a Roman who carried on the ideas of earlier Greek atomists, wrote:

> The light and heat of the sun; these are composed of minute atoms which, when they are shoved off, lose no time in shooting right across the interspace of air in the direction imparted by the shove.
>
> *–Lucretius, on the nature of the Universe*

Despite being similar to later particle theories of light, Lucretius's views were not generally accepted and light was still theorized as emanating from the eye.

In his *Catoptrica*, Hero of Alexandria showed by a geometrical method that the actual path taken by a ray of light reflected from a plane mirror is shorter than any other reflected path that might be drawn between the source and point of observation.

In a twelfth-century translation assigned to Roman mathematician Claudius Ptolemy, a study of refraction, including atmospheric refraction, was described. It was suggested that the angle of refraction is proportional to the angle of incidence.

Later in 499, Aryabhata, who proposed a heliocentric solar system of gravitation in his *Aryabhatiya*, wrote that the planets and the Moon do not have their own light but reflect the light of the Sun.

The Indian Buddhists, such as Dignaga in the 5th century and Dharmakirti in the 7th century, developed a type of atomism that is a philosophy about reality being composed of atomic entities that are momentary flashes of light or energy. They viewed light as being an atomic entity equivalent to energy, similar to the modern concept of photons, though they also viewed all matter as being composed of these light/energy particles.

The Beginnings of Geometrical Optics

The early writers discussed here treated vision more as a geometrical than as a physical, physiological, or psychological problem. The first known author of a treatise on geometrical optics was the geometer Euclid (c. 325 BC-265 BC). Euclid began his study of optics as he began his study of geometry, with a set of self-evident axioms.

Lines (or visual rays) can be drawn in a straight line to the object.

- Those lines falling upon an object form a cone.
- Those things upon which the lines fall are seen.
- Those things seen under a larger angle appear larger.
- Those things seen by a higher ray, appear higher.
- Right and left rays appear right and left.
- Things seen within several angles appear clearer.

Euclid did not define the physical nature of these visual rays but, using the principles of geometry, he discussed the effects of perspective and the rounding of things seen at a distance.

Where Euclid had limited his analysis to simple direct vision, Hero of Alexandria (c. AD 10-70) extended the principles of geometrical optics to consider problems of reflection (catoptrics). Unlike Euclid, Hero occasionally commented on the physical nature of visual rays, indicating that they proceeded at great speed from the eye to the object seen and were reflected from smooth surfaces but could become trapped in the porosities of unpolished surfaces. This has come to be known as *emission theory*.

Hero demonstrated the equality of the angle of incidence and reflection on the grounds that this is the shortest path from the object to the observer. On this basis, he was able to define the fixed relation between an object and its image in a plane mirror. Specifically, the image appears to be as far behind the mirror as the object really is in front of the mirror.

Like Hero, Ptolemy (c. 90–c. 168) considered the visual rays as proceeding from the eye to the object seen, but, unlike Hero, considered that the visual rays were not discrete lines, but formed a continuous cone. Ptolemy extended the study of vision beyond direct and reflected vision; he also studied vision by refracted rays (dioptrics), when we see objects through the interface between two media of different density. He conducted experiments to measure the path of vision when we look from air to water, from air to glass, and from water to glass and tabulated the relationship between the incident and refracted rays.

His tabulated results have been studied for the air water interface, and in general the values he obtained reflect the theoretical refraction given by modern theory, but the outliers are distorted to represent Ptolemy's *a priori* model of the nature of refraction.

The Beginnings of Physical Optics

Ibn al-Haytham (known in as *Alhacen* or *Alhazen* in Western Europe) (965-1040), often regarded as the 'father of modern optics', formulated 'the first comprehensive and systematic alternative to Greek optical theories." He initiated a revolution in optics and visual perception also known as the 'Optical Revolution', and laid the foundations for a physical optics. Ibn al-Haytham's key achievement was two-fold: first, to insist that vision only occurred because of rays entering the eye and that rays postulated to proceed from the eye had nothing to do with it; the second was to define the physical nature of the rays discussed by earlier geometrical optical writers, considering them as the forms of light and colour. He developed a camera obscura to demonstrate that light and colour from different candles passed through a single aperture in straight lines, without intermingling at the aperture. He then analyzed these physical rays according to the principles of geometrical optics. Ibn al-Haytham also employed the experimental scientific method as a form of demonstration in optics. He wrote many books on optics, most significantly the *Book of Optics* (*Kitab al Manazir* in Arabic), translated into Latin as the *De aspectibus* or *Perspectiva*, which disseminated his ideas to Western Europe and had great influence on the later developments of optics.

Another aspect associated with Ibn al-Haytham's optical research is related to systemic and methodological reliance on experimentation (*i'tibar*) and controlled testing in his scientific inquiries. Moreover, his experimental directives rested on combining classical physics (*'ilm tabi'i*) with mathematics (*ta'alim*; geometry in particular) in terms of devising the rudiments of what may be designated as a hypothetico-deductive procedure in scientific research. This mathematical-physical approach to experimental science supported most of his propositions in *Kitab al-Manazir* (*The Optics*; *De aspectibus* or *Perspectivae*) and grounded his theories of vision, light and colour, as well as his research in catoptrics and dioptrics. His legacy was further advanced through the 'reforming' of his *Optics* by Kamal al-Din al-Farisi (d. ca. 1320) in the latter's *Kitab Tanqih al-Manazir* (*The Revision of* [Ibn al-Haytham's] *Optics*). The *Book of Optics* established experimentation as the norm of proof in optics, and gave optics a physico-mathematical conception at a much earlier date than the other mathematical disciplines of astronomy and mechanics. The book was influential in both the Islamic world and in Western Europe.

Avicenna (980-1037) agreed with Alhazen that the speed of light is finite, as he "observed that if the perception of light is due to the emission of some sort of particles by a luminous source, the speed of light must be finite." Abu Rayhan al-Biruni (973-1048) also agreed that light has a finite speed, and he was the first to discover that the speed of light is much faster than the speed of sound.

Abu 'Abd Allah Muhammad ibn Ma'udh, who lived in Al-Andalus during the second half of the 11th century, wrote a work on optics later translated into Latin as *Liber de crepisculis*, which was mistakenly attributed to Alhazen. This was a "short work containing an estimation of the angle of depression of the sun at the beginning of the morning twilight and at the end of the evening twilight, and an attempt to calculate on the basis of this and other data the height of the atmospheric moisture responsible for the refraction of the sun's rays." Through his experiments, he obtained the value of 18°, which comes close to the modern value.

In the late 13th and early 14th centuries, Qutb al-Din al-Shirazi (1236-1311) and his student Kamal al-Din al-Farisi (1260-1320) continued the work of Ibn al-Haytham, and they were the first to give the correct explanations for the rainbow phenomenon. Al-Farisi published his findings in his *Kitab Tanqih al-Manazir* (*The Revision of* [Ibn al-Haytham's] *Optics*).

In 1574, Taqi al-Din (1526–1585) wrote the last major Arabic work on optics, entitled *Kitab Nur hadaqat al-ibsar wa-nur haqiqat al-anzar* (*Book of the Light of the Pupil of Vision and the Light of the Truth of the Sights*), which contains experimental investigations in three volumes on vision, the light's reflection, and the light's refraction. The book deals with the structure of light, its diffusion and global refraction, and the relation between light and colour. In the first volume, he discusses "the nature of light, the source of light, the nature of the propagation of light, the formation of sight, and the effect of light on the eye and sight". In the second volume, he provides "experimental proof of the specular reflection of accidental as well as essential light, a complete formulation of the laws of reflection, and a description of the construction and use of a copper instrument for measuring reflections from plane, spherical, cylindrical, and conical mirrors, whether convex or concave." The third volume "analyses the important question of the variations light undergoes while travelling in media having different densities, i.e. the nature of refracted light, the formation of refraction, the nature of images formed by refracted light." He also describes what may be a rudimentary telescope.

The Beginnings of Physiological Optics

Ibn al-Haytham discussed the topics of medicine and ophthalmology in the anatomical and physiological portions of the *Book of Optics* and in his commentaries on Galenic works. He accurately described the process of sight, the structure of the eye, image formation in the eye and the visual system. He also discovered the underlying principles of Hering's law of equal innervation, vertical horopters and binocular disparity and improved on the theories of binocular vision, motion perception and horopters previously discussed by Aristotle, Euclid and Ptolemy.

He discussed ocular anatomy, and was the first author to deal with the 'descriptive anatomy' and 'functional anatomy' of the eye independently. Much of his decriptive anatomy was faithful to Galen's gross anatomy, but with significant differences in his approach. For example, the whole area of the eye behind the iris constitutes what Ibn al-Haytham uniquely called the *uveal sphere*, and his description of the eye was devoid of any teleological or humoral theories associated with Galenic anatomy. He also described the eye as being made up of two intersecting globes, which was essential to his functional anatomy of the eye.

After describing the construction of the eye, Ibn al-Haytham makes his most original anatomical contribution in describing the functional anatomy of the eye as an optical system, or optical instrument. His multiple light-source experiment via a reduction slit with the camera obscura, also known as the lamp experiment, provided sufficient empirical grounds for him to develop his theory of corresponding point projection of light from the surface of an object to form an image on a screen. It was his comparison between the eye and the beam-chamber, or *camera obscura*, which brought about his synthesis of anatomy and optics, giving rise to a new field of optics now known as "physiological optics". As he conceptualized the essential principles of pinhole projection from his experiments with the pinhole camera, he considered image inversion to also occur in the eye, and viewed the pupil as being similar to an aperture. Regarding the process of image formation, however, he incorrectly agreed with Avicenna that the lens was the receptive organ of sight, but correctly hinted at the retina also being involved in the process.

Optics in Mediaeval Europe

The English bishop, Robert Grosseteste (c. 1175-1253), wrote on a wide range of scientific topics at the time of the origin of the mediaeval university and the recovery of the works of Aristotle. Grosseteste reflected a period of transition between the Platonism of early mediaeval learning and the new Aristotelianism, hence he tended to apply mathematics and the Platonic metaphor of light in many of his writings. He has been credited with discussing light from four different perspectives: an epistemology of light, a metaphysics or cosmogony of light, an etiology or physics of light, and a theology of light.

Setting aside the issues of epistemology and theology, Grosseteste's cosmogony of light describes the origin of the universe in what may loosely be described as a mediaeval 'big bang' theory. Both his biblical commentary, the *Hexaemeron* (1230 × 35), and his scientific *On Light*

(1235 × 40), took their inspiration from Genesis 1:3, 'God said, let there be light', and described the subsequent process of creation as a natural physical process arising from the generative power of an expanding (and contracting) sphere of light.

His more general consideration of light as a primary agent of physical causation appears in his *On Lines, Angles, and Figures* where he asserts that "a natural agent propagates its power from itself to the recipient" and in *On the Nature of Places* where he notes that "every natural action is varied in strength and weakness through variation of lines, angles and figures."

The English Franciscan, Roger Bacon (c. 1214-1294) was strongly influenced by Grosseteste's writings on the importance of light. In his optical writings (the *Perspectiva*, the *De multiplicatione specierum*, and the *De speculis comburentibus*) he cited a wide range of recently translated optical and philosophical works, including those of Alhacen, Aristotle, Avicenna, Averroes, Euclid, al-Kindi, Ptolemy, Tideus, and Constantine the African. Although he was not a slavish imitator, he drew his mathematical analysis of light and vision from the writings of the Arabic writer, Alhacen. But he added to this the Neoplatonic concept, perhaps drawn from Grosseteste, that every object radiates a power (*species*) by which it acts upon nearby objects suited to receive those *species*. Note that Bacon's optical use of the term '*species*' differs significantly from the genus/species categories found in Aristotelian philosophy.

Another English Franciscan, John Pecham (died 1292) built on the work of Bacon, Grosseteste, and a diverse range of earlier writers to produce what became the most widely used textbook on Optics of the Middle Ages, the *Perspectiva communis*. His book centered on the question of vision, on how we see, rather than on the nature of light and colour. Pecham followed the model set forth by Alhacen, but interpreted Alhacen's ideas in the manner of Roger Bacon.

Like his predecessors, Witelo (c. 1230 × 1280 × 1314) drew on the extensive body of optical works recently translated from Greek and Arabic to produce a massive presentation of the subject entitled the *Perspectiva.* His theory of vision follows Alhacen and he does not consider Bacon's concept of *species*, although passages in his work demonstrate that he was influenced by Bacon's ideas. Judging from the number of surviving manuscripts, his work was not as influential as those of Pecham and Bacon, yet his importance, and that of Pecham, grew with the invention of printing.

Renaissance and Early Modern Optics

Johannes Kepler (1571-1630) picked up the investigation of the laws of optics from his lunar essay of 1600. Both lunar and solar eclipses presented unexplained phenomena, such as unexpected shadow sizes, the red colour of a total lunar eclipse, and the reportedly unusual light surrounding a total solar eclipse. Related issues of atmospheric refraction applied to all astronomical observations. Through most of 1603, Kepler paused his other work to focus on optical theory; the resulting manuscript, presented to the emperor on January 1, 1604, was published as *Astronomiae Pars Optica* (*The Optical Part of Astronomy*). In it, Kepler described the inverse-square law governing the intensity of light, reflection by flat and curved mirrors, and principles of pinhole cameras, as well as the astronomical implications of optics such as parallax and the apparent sizes of heavenly bodies. *Astronomiae Pars Optica* is generally recognized as the foundation of modern optics (though the law of refraction is conspicuously absent).

Willebrord Snellius (1580-1626) found the mathematical law of refraction, now known as Snell's law, in 1621. Subsequently René Descartes (1596-1650) showed, by using geometric construction and the law of refraction (also known as Descartes' law), that the angular radius of a rainbow is 42° (i.e. the angle subtended at the eye by the edge of the rainbow and the ray passing from the sun through the rainbow's centre is 42°). He also independently discovered the law of reflection, and his essay on optics was the first published mention of this law.

Christiaan Huygens (1629-1695) wrote several works in the area of optics. These included the *Opera reliqua* (also known as *Christiani Hugenii Zuilichemii, dum viveret Zelhemii toparchae, opuscula posthuma*) and the *Traitbe de la lumiaere.*

Isaac Newton (1643-1727) investigated the refraction of light, demonstrating that a prism could decompose white light into a spectrum of colours, and that a lens and a second prism could recompose the multicoloured spectrum into white light. He also showed that the coloured light does not change its properties by separating out a coloured beam and shining it on various objects. Newton noted that regardless of whether it was reflected or scattered or transmitted, it stayed the same colour. Thus, he observed that colour is the result of objects interacting with already-coloured light rather than objects generating the colour themselves. This is known as *Newton's theory of colour.* From this work he concluded that any refracting telescope would suffer from the dispersion of light into colours, and invented a reflecting telescope (today known as a Newtonian telescope) to bypass that problem. By grinding his own mirrors, using Newton's rings to judge the quality of the optics for his telescopes, he was able to produce a superior instrument to the refracting telescope, due primarily to the wider diameter of the mirror. In 1671 the Royal Society asked for a demonstration of his reflecting telescope. Their interest encouraged him to publish his notes *On Colour*, which he later expanded into his *Opticks.* Newton argued that light is composed of particles or *corpuscles* and were refracted by accelerating toward the denser medium, but he had to associate them with waves to explain the diffraction of light (*Opticks* Bk. II, Props. XII-L). Later physicists instead favoured a purely wavelike explanation of light to account for diffraction. Today's quantum mechanics, photons and the idea of wave-particle duality bear only a minor resemblance to Newton's understanding of light.

In his *Hypothesis of Light* of 1675, Newton posited the existence of the ether to transmit forces between particles. In 1704, Newton published *Opticks*, in which he expounded his corpuscular theory of light. He considered light to be made up of extremely subtle corpuscles, that ordinary matter was made of grosser corpuscles and speculated that through a kind of alchemical transmutation "Are not gross Bodies and Light convertible into one another, . . . and may not Bodies receive much of their Activity from the Particles of Light which enter their Composition?"

The Beginnings of Diffractive Optics

The effects of diffraction of light were first carefully observed and characterized by Francesco Maria Grimaldi, who also coined the term *diffraction*, from the Latin *diffringere*, 'to break into pieces', referring to light breaking up into different directions. The results of Grimaldi's observations were published posthumously in 1665. saac Newton studied these effects and attributed them to *inflexion* of light rays. James Gregory (1638-1675) observed the diffraction patterns caused by a bird feather, which was effectively the first diffraction grating. In 1803 Thomas Young did his famous experiment observing interference from two closely spaced slits. Explaining his results by interference of the waves emanating from the two different slits, he deduced that light must propagate as waves. Augustin-Jean Fresnel did more definitive studies and calculations of diffraction, published in 1815 and 1818, and thereby gave great support to the wave theory of light that had been advanced by Christiaan Huygens and reinvigorated by Young, against Newton's particle theory.

Lenses and Lensmaking

The earliest known lenses were made from polished crystal, often quartz, and have been dated as early as 700 BC for Assyrian lenses such as the Layard/Nimrud lens. There are many similar lenses from ancient Egypt, Greece and Babylon. The ancient Romans and Greeks filled glass spheres with water to make lenses.

Glass lenses were not thought of until the Middle Ages. Ibn al-Haytham (Alhacen) wrote about the effects of pinhole and concave lenses in his *Book of Optics*, which was influential in the development of the modern telescope. The earliest evidence of "a magnifying device, a convex lens forming a magnified image," also dates back to his *Book of Optics*. Roger Bacon used parts of glass spheres as magnifying glasses and recommended them to be used to help people read. Roger Bacon got his inspiration from Alhacen in the 11th century. He discovered that light reflects from objects and does not get released from them. Around 1284 in Italy, Salvino D'Armate is credited with inventing the first wearable eye glasses.

Between the 11th and 13th century 'reading stones' were invented. Often used by monks to assist in illuminating manuscripts, these were primitive plano-convex lenses initially made by cutting a glass sphere in half. As the stones were experimented with, it was slowly understood that shallower lenses magnified more effectively.

There is some documentary evidence, but no surviving designs or physical evidence, that the principles of telescopes were known in the late 16th century. Leonard Digges, Taqi al-Din and Giambattista della Porta independently developed rudimentary telescopes in the 1570s and 1580s. However, the earliest known working telescopes were the refracting telescopes that appeared in the Netherlands in 1608. Their development is credited to three individuals: Hans Lippershey and Zacharias Janssen, who were spectacle makers in Middelburg, and Jacob Metius of

Alkmaar. Galileo greatly improved upon these designs the following year. Isaac Newton is credited with constructing the first functional reflecting telescope in 1668, his Newtonian reflector.

The first microscope was made around 1595 in Middleburg, Holland. Three different eyeglass makers have been given credit for the invention: Hans Lippershey (who also developed the first real telescope); Hans Janssen; and his son, Zacharias. The coining of the name 'microscope' has been credited to Giovanni Faber, who gave that name to Galileo Galilei's compound microscope in 1625.

Quantum Optics

Light is made up of particles called photons and hence inherently is quantized. Quantum optics is the study of the nature and effects of light as quantized photons. The first indication that light might be quantized came from Max Planck in 1899 when he correctly modelled blackbody radiation by assuming that the exchange of energy between light and matter only occurred in discrete amounts he called quanta. It was unknown whether the source of this discreteness was the matter or the light. In 1905, Albert Einstein published the theory of the photoelectric effect. It appeared that the only possible explanation for the effect was the quantization of light itself. Later, Niels Bohr showed that atoms could only emit discrete amounts of energy. The understanding of the interaction between light and matter following from these developments not only formed the basis of quantum optics but also were crucial for the development of quantum mechanics as a whole. However, the subfields of quantum mechanics dealing with matter-light interaction were principally regarded as research into matter rather than into light and hence, one rather spoke of atom physics and quantum electronics.

This changed with the invention of the maser in 1953 and the laser in 1960. Laser science — research into principles, design and application of these devices — became an important field, and the quantum mechanics underlying the laser's principles was studied now with more emphasis on the properties of light, and the name *quantum optics* became customary.

As laser science needed good theoretical foundations, and also because research into these soon proved very fruitful, interest in quantum optics rose. Following the work of Dirac in quantum field theory, George Sudarshan, Roy J. Glauber, and Leonard Mandel applied quantum theory to the electromagnetic field in the 1950s and 1960s to gain a more detailed understanding of photodetection and the statistics of light (see degree of coherence). This led to the introduction of the coherent state as a quantum description of laser light and the realization that some states of light could not be described with classical waves. In 1977, Kimble et al. demonstrated the first source of light which required a quantum description: a single atom that emitted one photon at a time. Another quantum state of light with certain advantages over any classical state, squeezed light, was soon proposed. At the same time, development of short and ultrashort laser pulses — created by Q-switching and mode-locking techniques — opened the way to the study of unimaginably fast ('ultrafast') processes. Applications for solid state research (e.g. Raman spectroscopy) were found, and mechanical forces of light on matter were studied. The latter led to levitating and positioning clouds of atoms or even small biological samples in an optical trap or optical tweezers by laser beam. This, along with Doppler cooling was the crucial technology needed to achieve the celebrated Bose-Einstein condensation.

Other remarkable results are the demonstration of quantum entanglement, quantum teleportation, and (recently, in 1995) quantum logic gates. The latter are of much interest in quantum information theory, a subject which partly emerged from quantum optics, partly from theoretical computer science.

Today's fields of interest among quantum optics researchers include parametric down-conversion, parametric oscillation, even shorter (attosecond) light pulses, use of quantum optics for quantum information, manipulation of single atoms, Bose-Einstein condensates, their application, and how to manipulate them (a sub-field often called atom optics), and much more.

Research into quantum optics that aims to bring photons into use for information transfer and computation is now often called photonics to emphasize the claim that photons and photonics will take the role that electrons and electronics now have.

10

Stained Glass

The term *stained glass* can refer to the material of coloured glass or the craft of working with it. Throughout its thousand-year history, the term 'stained glass' has been applied almost exclusively to the windows of churches and other significant buildings. Although traditionally made in flat panels and used as windows, the creations of modern stained glass artists also include three-dimensional structures and sculpture.

Modern vernacular usage has often extended the term 'stained glass' to include domestic leadlight and objets d'art created from lead came and copper foil glasswork exemplified in the famous lamps of Louis Comfort Tiffany.

As a material *stained glass* is glass that has been coloured by adding metallic salts during its manufacture. The coloured glass is crafted into *stained glass windows* in which small pieces of glass are arranged to form patterns or pictures, held together (traditionally) by strips of lead and supported by a rigid frame. Painted details and yellow stain are often used to enhance the design. The term *stained glass* is also applied to windows in which the colours have been painted onto the glass and then fused to the glass in a kiln.

Stained glass, as an art and a craft, requires the artistic skill to conceive an appropriate and workable design, and the engineering skills to assemble the piece. A window must fit snugly into the space for which it is made, must resist wind and rain, and also, especially in the larger windows, must support its own weight. Many large windows have withstood the test of time and remained substantially intact since the late Middle Ages. In Western Europe they constitute the major form of pictorial art to have survived. In this context, the purpose of a stained glass window is not to allow those within a building to see the world outside or even primarily to admit light but rather to control it. For this reason stained glass windows have been described as 'illuminated wall decorations'.

The design of a window may be non-figurative or figurative; may incorporate narratives drawn from the Bible, history, or literature; may represent saints or patrons, or use symbolic motifs, in particular armorial. Windows within a building may be thematic, for example: within a churc — episodes from the life of Christ; within a parliament building — shields of the constituencies; within a college hall — figures representing the arts and sciences; or within a home — flora, fauna, or landscape.

Glass Production

From the 10th or 11th century, when stained glass began to flourish as an art, glass factories were set up where there was a ready supply of silica, the essential product of glass manufacture. Glass was usually coloured by adding metallic oxides to the glass while in a molten state in a clay pot over a furnace. Glass coloured in this way was known as *pot metal.* Copper oxides were added to produce green, cobalt for blue, and gold was added to produce red glass. Much modern red glass is produced using ingredients less expensive than gold and giving a brighter red of a more vermilion shade.

Cylinder Glass: This glass was collected from the pot into a molten ball and blown, while being continually manipulated until it formed a large cylindrical bottle shape of even diameter and wall-thickness. It was then cut open, laid flat and annealed to make it stable. This is the type of glass most commonly used for ancient stained glass windows.

Crown Glass: This glass was partly blown into a hollow vessel, then put onto a revolving table which could be rapidly spun like a potter's wheel. The centrifugal force caused the molten material to flatten and spread outwards. It could then be cut into small sheets. This glass could be made coloured and used for stained glass windows, but is typically associated with small paned windows of 16th and 17th century houses. The concentric, curving ripples are characteristic of this process. The center of each piece of glass received less force during the spinning, and thus produced was a thicker piece. These centres were for the special effect created by their lumpy, refractive quality. They are known as *bull's eyes* and are feature of late 19th century domestic leadlight and are sometimes also used with *cathedral glass* or *quarry glass* in non-pictorial church windows of that date.

Table Glass: This glass was produced by pouring molten glass onto a metal table and sometimes rolling it with a large metal cylinder. The glass thus produced is heavily textured by the reaction of the glass with the cold metal. Glass of this appearance is commercially produced and widely used today, under the name of cathedral glass, although it was not the type of glass favoured for stained glass in ancient cathedrals. It has been much used for lead lighting in churches in the 20th century. Modern glass made by this technique is often heavily patterned by the use of an engrave metal roller.

Flashed Glass: Red pot metal glass was often undesirably dark in colour and prohibitively expensive. The method developed to produce red glass was called *flashing*. In this procedure, a semi-molten cylinder of clear glass was dipped into a pot of red glass so that the red glass formed a thin coating. The laminated glass thus formed was cut, flattened and heat annealed.

There are a number of advantages to this technique. It allows a variety in the depth of red ranging from very dark and almost opaque, through ruby red to pale and sometimes streaky red that was often used for thin border pieces. The other advantage was that the red of double-layered glass could be engraved or abraded to allow light to shine through the clear glass underneath. In the late Medieval period, this method was often employed to add rich patterns to the robes of Saints. The other advantage, much exploited by late Victorian and early 20th century artists, was that sheets could be flashed in which the depth of colour varied across the sheet. This was applied to a range of colours. Some stained glass studios, notably Lavers, Barraud and Westlake in England, made extensive use of large segments of irregularly flashed glass in robes and draperies.

Modern Production of Traditional Glass: There are a number of glass factories, notably in Germany, USA, England, France, Poland and Russia, which produce high quality glass by traditional methods. Such glass is produced primarily for the restoration of older windows from 1920s and before. The production of new windows in traditional Victorian, Arts and Crafts and early 20th century styles often uses traditional glass. Modern stained glass windows also often use a variety of these different types of glass, or employ commercially made glass.

Creating Stained Glass Windows

The first stage in the production of a window is to make, or acquire from the architect or owners of the building, an accurate template of the window opening that the glass is to fit.

The subject matter of the window is determined to suit the location, a particular theme, or the whim of the patron. A small design called a *Vidimus* is prepared which can be shown to the patron.

A traditional narrative window has panels which relate a story. A figurative window could have rows of saints or dignitaries. Scriptural texts or mottoes are sometimes included and perhaps the names of the patrons or the person as whose memorial the window is dedicated. In a window of a traditional type, it is usually at the discretion of the designer to fill the surrounding areas with borders, floral motifs and canopies.

A full sized cartoon is drawn for every 'light' (opening) of the window. A small church window might typically be of two lights, with some simple *tracery* lights above. A large window might have four or five lights. The east or west window of a large cathedral might have seven lights in three *tiers* with elaborate tracery. In Mediaeval times the cartoon was drawn straight onto a whitewashed table, which was then used for cutting, painting and assembling the window.

The designer must take into account the design, the structure of the window, the nature and size of the glass available and his or her own preferred technique. The cartoon is then be divided into a patchwork as a template for each small glass piece. The exact position of the lead which holds the glass in place is part of the calculated visual effect. Each piece of glass is selected for the desired colour and cut to match a section of the template. An exact fit is ensured by *grozing* the edges with a tool which can nibble off small pieces. Details of faces, hair and hands can be painted onto the inner surface of the glass in a special glass paint which contains finely ground lead or copper filings, ground glass, gum arabic and a medium such as wine, vinegar or (traditionally) urine. The art of painting details became increasingly elaborate and reached its height in the early 20th century. Once the window is cut and painted, the pieces are assembled by slotting them into H-sectioned lead *cames*. The joints are then all soldered together and the glass pieces are stopped from rattling and the window made weatherproof by forcing a soft oily cement or *mastic* between the glass and the cames. Traditionally, when the windows were inserted into the window spaces, iron rods were put across at various points, to support the weight of the window, which was tied to the rods by copper wire. Some very large early Gothic windows are divided into sections by heavy metal frames called *ferramenta*. This method of support was also favoured for large, usually painted, windows of the Baroque period. From 1300 onwards, artists started using *silver stain* which was made with silver nitrate. It gave a yellow effect ranging from pale lemon to deep orange. It was usually painted onto the outside of a piece of glass, then fired to make it permanent. This yellow was particularly useful for enhancing borders, canopies and haloes, and turning blue glass into green glass for green grass. By about 1450 a stain known as *Cousin's rose* was used to enhance flesh tones. In the 1500s a range of glass stains were introduced, most of them coloured by ground glass particles. They were a form of enamel. Painting on glass with these stains was initially used for small heraldic designs and other details. By the 1600s a style of stained glass had evolved that was no longer dependent upon the skilful cutting of coloured glass into sections. Scenes were painted onto glass panels of square format, like tiles. The colours were annealed to the glass and the pieces were assembled into metal frames. In modern windows, copper foil is now sometimes used instead of lead. For further technical details, see Lead came and copper foil glasswork. In the late 19th and 20th centuries there have been many innovations in techniques and in the types of glass used. Many new types of glass have been developed for use in stained glass windows, in particular Tiffany glass and slab glass.

Origins

Coloured glass has been produced since ancient times. Both the Egyptians and the Romans excelled at the manufacture of small coloured glass objects. The British Museum holds two of the finest Roman pieces, the Lycurgus Cup, which is a murky mustard colour but glows purple-red to transmitted light, and the Portland vase which is midnight blue, with a carved white overlay.

In Early Christian churches of the 4th and 5th centuries there are many remaining windows which are filled with ornate patterns of thinly-sliced alabaster set into wooden frames, giving a stained-glass like effect. Evidence of stained glass windows in churches and monasteries within Britain can be found as early as the 7th century. Benedict Biscop's monasteries in Monkwearmouth and Jarrow have revealed hundreds of pieces of coloured glass and lead from as early as 680 CE. Stained glass was also used by Islamic architects in Southwest Asia by the 8th century, when the alchemist Geber, in *Kitab al-Durra al-Maknuna*, gives 46 original recipes for producing coloured glass and describes the production of cutting glass into artificial gemstones.

Stained glass, as an art form, reached its height in the Middle Ages when it became a major pictorial form and was used to illustrate the narratives of the Bible to a largely illiterate populace.

In the Romanesque and Early Gothic period, from about 950 AD to 1240 AD, the untraceried windows demanded large expanses of glass which of necessity were supported by robust iron frames, such as may be seen at Chartres Cathedral and at the eastern end of Canterbury Cathedral. As Gothic architecture developed into a more ornate form, windows grew larger, affording greater illumination to the interiors, but were divided into sections by vertical shafts and tracery of stone. The elaboration of form reached its height of complexity in the Flamboyant style in Europe and windows grew still larger with the development of the Perpendicular style in England.

Integrated with the *lofty verticals* of Gothic cathedrals and parish churches, the glass designs became more daring. The circular form, or rose window developed in France from relatively simple windows with pierced openings through slabs of thin stone to wheel windows, as exemplified by that in the West front of Chartres Cathedral, and ultimately to designs of enormous complexity, the tracery being drafted from hundreds of different points, such as those at Sainte-Chapelle, Paris and the 'Bishop's Eye' at Lincoln Cathedral.

The Renaissance and Reformation

In Europe, stained glass continued to be produced with the style evolving from the Gothic to the Classical style, which is widely represented in Germany, Belgium and the Netherlands, despite the rise of Protestantism. In France, much glass of this period was produced at the Limoges factory, and in Italy at Murano, where stained glass and faceted lead crystal are often coupled together in the same window. Ultimately, the French Revolution brought about the neglect or destruction of many windows in France. At the Reformation, in England large numbers of Mediaeval and Renaissance windows were smashed and replaced with plain glass. The Dissolution of the Monasteries under Henry VIII and the injunctions of Oliver Cromwell against "abused images" (the object of veneration) resulted in the loss of thousands of windows. Few remain undamaged; of them the windows in the private chapel at Hengrave Hall in Suffolk are among the finest. With the latter wave of destruction the traditional methods of working with stained glass died and were not to be rediscovered in England until the early 19th century.

Revival in Britain

The Catholic revival in England, gaining force in the early 19th century, with its renewed interest in the mediaeval church brought a revival of church building in the Gothic style, claimed by John Ruskin to be 'the true Catholic style'. The architectural movement was led by Augustus Welby Pugin. Many new churches were planted in large towns and many old churches were restored. This brought about a great demand for the revival of the art of stained glass window making.

Among the earliest 19th century English manufacturers and designers are William Warrington and

John Hardman of Birmingham whose nephew, John Hardman Powell, who had a commercial eye and exhibited works at the Philadelphia Exhibition of 1873, influencing stained glass in the United States of America. Other manufacturers include William Wailes, Ward and Hughes, Clayton and Bell, Heaton, Butler and Bayne and Charles Eamer Kempe. A Scottish designer, Daniel Cottier, opened firms in Australia and the US.

Revival in France

In France there was a greater continuity of stained glass production than in England. In the early 19th century most stained glass was made of large panes that were extensively painted and fired, the designs often being copied directly from oil paintings by famous artists. In 1824 the Sèvres Porcelain factory began producing stained glass to supply the increasing demand. In France many churches and cathedrals suffered despoilation during the French Revolution. During the 19th century a great number of churches were restored by Viollet-le-Duc. Many of France's finest ancient windows were restored at this time. From 1839 onwards much stained glass was produced that very closely imitates medieval glass, both in the artwork and in the nature of the glass itself. The pioneers were Henri Gèrente and Andre Lusson. Other glass was designed in a more Classical manner, and characterised by the brilliant cerulean colour of the blue backgrounds (as against the purple-blue of the glass of Chartres) and the use of pink and mauve glass.

Revival in Europe

During the mid to late 19th century, many of Germany's ancient buildings were restored, and some, such as Cologne Cathedral were completed in the mediaeval style. There was a great demand for stained glass. The designs for many windows were based directly on the work of famous engravers such as Albrecht Dürer. Original designs often imitate this style. Much 19th century German glass has large sections of painted detail rather than outlines and details dependent on the lead. The Royal Bavarian Glass painting Studio was founded by Ludwig I in 1827. A major firm was Mayer of Munich which commenced glass production in 1860, and is still operating as *Franz Mayer of Munich, Inc.*. German stained glass found a market across Europe, in America and Australia. Stained glass studios were also founded in Italy and Belgium at this time.

Twentieth Century

Many 19th-century firms failed early in the twentieth century as the Gothic movement had been superseded by newer styles. At the same time there were also some interesting developments where stained glass artists took studios in shared facilities. Examples include the Glass House in London set up by Mary Lowndes and A.J. Drury and An Túr Gloine in Dublin, which was run by Sarah Purser.

A revival occurred in the middle of the century because of the desire to restore the thousands of church windows throughout Europe, destroyed as a result of bombing during the World War II. German artists led the way. Much work of the period is mundane and often was not made by its designers but industrially produced.

Other artists sought to transform an ancient art form into a contemporary one, sometimes using only traditional techniques but often exploring the medium of glass in different ways and in combination with different materials. The use of slab glass set in concrete was another 20th-century innovation. Gemmail, a technique developed by the French artist Jean Crotti in 1936 and perfected in the 1950s, is a type of stained glass where adjacent pieces of glass are overlapped, without using lead nervures to join the pieces, allowing for a greater diversity and subtlety of colour. Many famous works by late 19th- and early 20th-century painters, notably Picasso, have been reproduced in gemmail. A major exponent of this technique is the German artist Walter Womacka.

Among the early well-known 20th-century artists who experimented with stained glass as an Abstract art form were Theo van Doesburg and Piet Mondrian. In the 1960s and 70s the Expressionist painter Marc Chagall produced designs for many stained glass windows that are intensely coloured and crammed with symbolic details. Important 20th-century stained glass artists include Douglas Strachan, Ervin Bossanyi, Louis Davis,Wilhelmina Geddes, Karl Parsons, Patrick Reyntiens, Ludwig Schaffrath, Johannes Shreiter, Judith Schaechter, Paul Woodroffe, Jean René Bazaine at Saint Séverin and the Loire Studio of Gabriel Loire at Chartres. The Luxus Keibel studio in Mexico specialises in domestic stained glass in both contemporary and 19th century styles. The west windows of England's Manchester Cathedral, by Tony Hollaway, are some of the most notable examples of symbolic work.

In the US, there is a 100-year-old trade organization, The Stained Glass Association of America, whose purpose is to function as a publicly recognized organization to assure survival of the craft by offering guidelines, instruction and training to craftspersons. The SGAA also sees its role as defending and protecting its craft against regulations that might restrict its freedom as an architectural art form. The current president is B. Gunar Gruenke of the Conrad Schmitt Studios. Today there are academic establishments that teach the traditional skills. One of these is Florida State University's Master Craftsman Programme who recently completed a 30 ft high stained-glass windows installed in Bobby Bowden Field at Doak Campbell Stadium.

11

Glass in Islamic Culture

The influence of the Islamic world to the history of glass is reflected by its distribution around the world, from Europe to China, and from Russia to East Africa. Islamic glass developed a unique expression that was characterized by the introduction of new techniques and the innovation of old traditions.

Islamic glass did not begin to develop a recognizable expression until the late 8th or early 9th century AD, despite Islam spreading across the Middle East and North Africa during the mid-7th century AD. Despite bringing enormous religious and socio-political changes to the region, this event appears to have not drastically effected the day-to-day workings of craft industries, nor did it cause "extensive destruction or long-lasting disruption". The Roman (Levant and Egypt) and Sassanian (Persia and Mesopotamia) glassmaking industries continued in much the same way they had for centuries earlier. Following the unification of the entire region, the interaction of ideas and techniques was facilitated, allowing for the fusion of these two separate traditions with new ideas, ultimately leading to the Islamic glass industry. Roman glassmaking traditions that are important in the Islamic period include the application of glass trails as a surface embellishment, while stylistic techniques adopted from the Sassanian Empire include various styles of glass cutting. This may have developed out of the long-standing hardstone carving traditions in Persia and Mesopotamia. In regards to glassmaking technology, tank furnaces used in the Levant to produce slabs of raw glass for export during the Classical Period were used during the Early Islamic Period in the same region until the 10th or 11th centuries AD.

Technological Change

During the first centuries of Islamic rule, glassmakers in the Eastern Mediterranean continued to use the Roman recipe consisting of calcium-rich sand (providing the silica and lime) and mineral natron (soda component) from the Wadi el-Natrun in Egypt, and examples of natron-based Islamic glass have been found in the Levant up to the late 9th century AD. Archaeological evidence has shown that the use of natron ceased, and plant ash became the source of soda for all Islamic glass in the following centuries. The reasons for this technological transition remain unclear, although it has been postulated that civil unrest in Egypt during the early 9th century AD led to a cut-off in the natron supply, thus forcing Islamic glassmakers to look for alternate soda sources. Evidence of experimentation with the basic glass recipe at Beth She'arim (modern Israel) during the early 9th century AD further supports this argument. A glass slab made from a tank mold from the site contained an excess amount of lime, and may be the result of mixing sand with plant ash. Whilst the raw glass would have been unusable due to its composition, it does suggest that at this time, Islamic glassmakers in the Levant were combining aspects of Sassanian and Roman traditions in an effort to solve the problem created by the lack of access to mineral natron. The use of plant ash, specifically from halophytic (salt-loving) plants, which were plentiful in the Middle East due to the climate, was well-known in Persia and Mesopotamia.

The glass industry in the Early Islamic Period can initially be characterized as a continuation of older traditions, coinciding with the Umayyad Caliphate, the first Islamic dynasty. Following the rise of the Abbasid Caliphate in 750 AD, the capital of the Islamic world was moved from Damascus in the Levant to Baghdad in Mesopotamia. This led to a cultural shift away from the influences of Classical traditions, and allowed for the development of an 'Islamic' expression.

The production of glass during this period is concentrated in three main regions of the Islamic world. Firstly, the Eastern Mediterranean remained a centre of glass production, as it had been for centuries. Excavations at Qal'at Sem'an in northern Syria, Tyre in Lebanon, Beth She'arim and Bet Eli'ezer in Israel and at Fustat (Old Cairo) in Egypt have all shown evidence for glass production, including numerous vessels, raw glass, and their associated furnaces. Also adding to our understanding of the glass industry in this region is the aforementioned shipwreck at Serçe Liman. In Persia, a formerly Sassanian region, archaeological activity has located a number of sites with large deposits of Early Islamic Glass, including Nishapur, Siraf, and Susa. Numerous kilns suggest Nishapur was an important production centre, whilst the identification of a local type of glass at Siraf suggests the same for that site. In Mesopotamia, excavations at Samarra, a temporary capital of the Abbasid Caliphate during the mid-9th century AD, produced a wide range of glass vessels, while work at al-Mada'in (former Ctesiphon) and Raqqa (on the Euphrates River in modern Syria) provide evidence for glass production in the region.

The majority of the decorative traditions used in the Early Islamic Period concerned the manipulation of the glass itself, and included trail-application, carving, and mold-blowing. As mentioned previously, glass-carving and trail application are a continuation of older techniques, the former associated with Sassanian glassmaking and the latter with Roman traditions. In relief cutting, a specialized form of glass-carving most often used on colourless and transparent glass, "the area surrounding the decorative elements was carved back to the ground, thus leaving the former in relief". Mold-blowing, based on older traditions, is another specialized technique that spread widely throughout the Islamic world during this period. Two distinct types of molds are known archaeologically; a two-part mold made up of separate halves, and the 'dip' mold, whereby the viscous glass is placed entirely inside one mold. The molds were often made of bronze, although there are examples of some being ceramic.

A final decorative technology that is a distinct marker of the Early Islamic Period is the use of lustre painting. While some scholars see this as a purely Islamic invention originating in Fustat, others place the origins of lustre decoration in Roman and Coptic Egypt during the centuries preceding the rise of Islam. Staining glass vessels with copper and silver pigments was known from around the 3rd century AD, although true lustre technology probably began sometime between the 4th and 8th centuries AD. Lustre painting on glass involves the application of copper and silver pigments, followed by a specific firing that allows for the ionic exchange of Ag^+ and Cu^+ with the glass, resulting in a metallic sheen fully bound to the vessel. Regardless of its specific origins, lustre decoration was a key technology in glass production that continued to develop throughout the Early Islamic Period, and spread not only geographically, but also to other material industries in the form of glazed ceramics.

Middle Islamic Glass: Late 12th to Late 14th Century AD

This is the 'Golden Age' of Islamic glassmaking, despite the fractious nature of the Islamic world. Persia and Mesopotamia (along with parts of Syria for some time) came under control of the Seljuq Turks, and later the Mongols, while in the Eastern Mediterranean, the Ayyubid and Mamluk Dynasties held sway. Furthermore, this period saw

European interruptions into the Middle East due to the Crusades. Glass production seemingly ceased to exist in Persia and Mesopotamia, and little is known about the reasons for this. However, in the earlier part of this period, there is evidence for glass-making in Central Asia, for example at Kuva in modern Uzbekistan. This tradition presumably ended with the Mongol invasions of the mid-thirteenth century AD that destroyed other sites in the region.

The glass-producing regions of Syria and Egypt continued their industries. It is for the materials excavated and produced at sites such as Samsat in southern Turkey, Aleppo and Damascus in Syria, Hebron in the Levant and Cairo that this period is referred to as the 'Golden Age' of Islamic glass. The Middle Islamic Period is characterized by the perfection of various polychrome decorative traditions, the most important of which are marvering, enamelling, and gilding, while relief-carving and lustre painting seemingly fell out of fashion. Marvering involves applying a continuous trail of opaque glass (in various colours such as white, red, yellow, or pale blue) around the body of a glass object. This trail may then be manipulated by pulling it, creating a characteristic 'wavy' pattern. The object was then rolled on a marver (a stone or iron slab) to work the trail into the glass vessel itself.

This technique, used on a variety of glass objects from bowls and bottles to chess pieces, was introduced around the late 12th century AD, but is in fact a revival of a much older glass-working tradition that has its origins in the Late Bronze Age in Egypt.

Gilding during this period involved applying small amounts of gold in suspension onto a glass body, followed by a low firing to fuse the two materials, and was adopted from Byzantine traditions. This technique was often combined with enamelling, the application of ground glass with a colourant, to traditional and new vessel forms, and represents the height of Islamic glassmaking. Enamelling, a resurrection of older techniques, was first practiced in the Islamic world at Raqqa (Syria) during the late 12th century, but also spread to Cairo during Mamluk rule. A study of various enamelled vessels, including beakers and mosque lamps, suggests that there are two subtle yet distinct firing practices, possibly representing two distinct production centres or glass-working traditions. Due to its high demand, enamelled glass was exported throughout the Islamic world, Europe, and China during this period. Enamelling eventually ended in Syria and Egypt following disruption by various Mongol invasions from the 13th through to the 15th centuries AD.

A final note on glass from the Middle Islamic Period is the increased interaction between the Middle East and Europe. The Crusades allowed for the European discovery of Islamic gilded and enamelled vessels. The 'Goblet of the Eight Princes' brought to France from the Levant is one of the earliest examples of this technique. Furthermore, large amounts of raw plant ash were exported solely to Venice, fuelling that city's glass industries. It was also in Venice that enamelling was resurrected following its decline in the Islamic world.

Late Islamic Glass: 15th to Mid 19th Century AD

The Late Islamic Period is dominated by three main empires and areas of glass production; the Ottomans in Turkey, the Safavid (and later the Zand and Qajar) Dynasty in Persia, and the Mughals in northern India. The most important over-riding characteristic of glass production in this period is the "direct influence of European glass" and, in particular, that of Venice, Bohemia (in the 18th century), and the Dutch. The production of high-quality fine glass essentially ended in Egypt, Syria, and Persia, and it was only in India during the 17th century that Islamic glass regained a high level of artistic expression following European influence.

Historical documents and accounts, such as the *Surname-i Humayun*, show the presence of glassmaking, and a glassmaker's guild, in Istanbul, as well as production at Beykoz on the coast of the Bosphorus, in the Ottoman Empire. The glass made at these centres was not of great quality and was highly influenced by Venetian and Bohemian styles and techniques. In Persia, evidence for glassmaking following the Mongol invasions of the 13th century does not reappear until the Safavid period (17th century). European travellers wrote accounts of glass factories in Shiraz, and it is thought that transplanted Italian craftsmen brought about this revival. No significant decorative treatments or technical characteristics of glass were introduced or revived during this period in Persia. Bottle and jug forms with simple applied or ribbed decoration, made from coloured transparent glass, were common, and are linked to the Shirazi wine industry.

Mughal glassmaking in India, on the other hand, saw a return to the enamelling and gilding traditions from the Middle Islamic Period, as well as the glass-carving techniques used in Persia during the earliest centuries of the Islamic world. Glass workshops and factories were initially found near the Mughal capital of Agra, Patna (eastern India), and in Gujarat province (western India), and by the 18th century had spread to other regions in western India. New forms were introduced using these older Islamic glass-working techniques, and of these, *nargileh* (water pipe) bases became the most dominant. Square bottles based on Dutch forms, decorated with enamelling and gilding in Indian motifs, are another important expression in Mughal glassmaking, and were produced at Bhuj, Kutch, and in Gujarat. Ethnographic study of current glass production in Jalesar shows fundamental similarities between this site and the Early Islamic tank furnaces found in the Levant, despite differences in the shape of the structures (round in India, rectangular at Bet She'arim), highlighting the technological continuity of the glass industry throughout the Islamic period.

Glass led contributed to a decline in the industry; however, utilitarian glass was still being made in the traditional centres.

The Roles of Islamic Glass

Whilst the various functions of Islamic glass have been touched upon during the previous discussion (mosque lamps from the Middle Islamic Period, wine bottles from Safavid Persia, *nargileh* bases from Mughal India), glass filled a multitude of roles throughout the history of the Islamic world. A variety of vessel forms used to hold a wide range of materials make up the bulk of glass objects (bowls, goblets, dishes, perfume bottles, etc.), and have seen the most attention from Islamic glass scholars. Some of the more distinct vessel functions from the Islamic period include inkwells, *qumqum* or perfume sprinklers, and vessels associated with Islamic science and medicine such as alembics, test-tubes, and cuppers. Glass was also used for aesthetic purposes in the form of decorative figurines and for jewellery as bracelets and beads. The bracelets, in particular, may prove to be an important archaeological tool in the dating of Islamic sites. Glass also filled various utilitarian roles, with evidence of use as windows and as coin weights. The variety of functions filled by glass and the sheer bulk of the material found through excavation further highlights its significance as a distinct and highly-developed material industry throughout the Islamic world.

Study of Islamic Glass

Islamic glass from this period has been given relatively little attention by scholars. One exception to this was the work carried out by Carl J. Lamm (1902-1987) . Lamm catalogued and classified the glass finds from important Islamic sites; for example Susa in Iran and at Samarra in Iraq. One of the most important discoveries in the field of Islamic glass was a shipwreck dated to around 1036 AD on the Turkey coast at Serçe Liman. The recovered cargo included vessel fragments and glass cullet exported from Syria. The significance of these finds lies in the information they can tell us about the production and distribution of Islamic glass. Despite this, the majority of studies have concentrated on stylistic and decorative classification and as such technological aspects of the industry, as well as undecorated vessels and objects, have often been overlooked within the field. This, in particular, is frustrating because the majority of glass finds during the Islamic period are undecorated and used for utilitarian purposes.

12

Mirror

A *mirror* is an object with at least one polished and therefore specularly reflective surface. The most familiar type of mirror is the plane mirror, which has a flat surface. Curved mirrors are also used, to produce magnified or diminished images or focus light or simply distort the reflected image.

Mirrors are commonly used for personal grooming (in which case the old-fashioned term 'looking-glass' can be used), decoration, and architecture. Mirrors are also used in scientific apparatus such as telescopes and lasers, cameras, and industrial machinery. Most mirrors are designed for visible light; however, mirrors designed for other types of waves or other wavelengths of electromagnetic radiation are also used, especially in non-optical instruments.

The first mirrors used by people were most likely pools of dark, still water, or water collected in a primitive vessel of some sort. The earliest manufactured mirrors were pieces of polished stone such as obsidian, a naturally occurring volcanic glass. Examples of obsidian mirrors found in Anatolia (modern-day Turkey) have been dated to around 6000 BC. Polished stone mirrors from central and south America date from around 2000 BC onwards. Mirrors of polished copper were crafted in Mesopotamia from 4000 BC, and in ancient Egypt from around 3000 BC. In China, bronze mirrors were manufactured from around 2000 BC, some of the earliest bronze and copper examples being produced by the Qijia culture. Mirrors made of other metal mixtures (alloys) such as copper and tin speculum metal may have also been produced in China and India. Mirrors of speculum metal or any precious metal were hard to produce and were only owned by the wealthy.

Metal-coated glass mirrors are said to have been invented in Sidon (modern-day Lebanon) in the first century AD, and glass mirrors backed with gold leaf are mentioned by the Roman author Pliny in his *Natural History*, written in about 77 AD. The Romans also developed a technique for creating crude mirrors by coating blown glass with molten lead.

Parabolic mirrors were described and studied in classical antiquity by the mathematician Diocles in his work *On Burning Mirrors*. Ptolemy conducted a number of experiments with curved polished iron mirrors, and discussed plane, convex spherical, and concave spherical mirrors in his *Optics*. Parabolic mirrors were also described by the physicist Ibn Sahl in the 10th century, and Ibn al-Haytham discussed concave and convex mirrors in both cylindrical and spherical geometries, carried out a number of experiments with mirrors, and solved the problem of finding the point on a convex mirror at which a ray coming from one point is reflected to another point. By the 11th century, clear glass mirrors were being produced in Moorish Spain.

Some time during the early Renaissance, European manufacturers perfected a superior method of coating glass with a tin-mercury amalgam. The exact date and location of the discovery is unknown, but in the 16th century, Venice, a city famed for its glass-making expertise, became a centre of mirror production using this new technique. Glass mirrors from this period were extremely expensive luxuries. The Saint-Gobain factory, founded by royal initiative in France, was an important manufacturer, and Bohemian and German glass, often rather cheaper, was also important.

The invention of the silvered-glass mirror is credited to German chemist Justus von Liebig in 1835 .His process involved the deposition of a thin layer of metallic silver onto glass through the chemical reduction of silver nitrate. This silvering process was adapted for mass manufacturing and led to the greater availability of affordable mirrors. Nowadays, mirrors are often produced by the vacuum deposition of aluminium (or sometimes silver) directly onto the glass substrate.

Manufacturing

Mirrors are manufactured by applying a reflective coating to a suitable substrate. The most common such substrate is glass, due to its transparency, ease of fabrication, rigidity, and ability to take a smooth finish. The reflective coating ('silver') is typically applied to the *back* surface of the glass, so that it is protected from corrosion and accidental damage. Glass is much more scratch-resistant than most substrates.

In classical antiquity mirrors were made of solid metal (bronze, later silver) and were too expensive for widespread use, as well as being prone to corrosion. Due to the low reflectivity of polished metal these mirrors also gave a darker image than modern ones, making them unsuitable for indoor use with the artificial lighting of the time (candles or lanterns).

The method of making mirrors out of plate glass was invented by 16th-century Venetian glassmakers on the island of Murano, who covered the back of the glass with mercury, obtaining near-perfect and undistorted reflection. For over one hundred years Venetian mirrors installed in richly decorated frames served as luxury decoration for palaces throughout Europe, but the secret of the mercury process eventually arrived to London and Paris during the 17th century, due to industrial espionage. French workshops succeeded in large scale industrialization of the process, eventually making mirrors affordable to the masses, although mercury's toxicity remained a problem.

In modern times the mirror substrate is shaped, polished and cleaned, and is then coated. Glass mirrors are most often coated with non-toxic silver or aluminium, implemented by a series of coatings.

The Tin(II) chloride is applied because silver will not bond with the glass. The activator causes the tin/silver to harden. Copper is added for long-term durability. The paint protects the coating on the back of the mirror from scratches and other accidental damage.

In some applications, generally those that are cost-sensitive or that require great durability, mirrors are made from a single, bulk material such as polished metal.

For technical applications such as laser mirrors, the reflective coating is typically applied by vacuum deposition on the *front* surface of the substrate. This eliminates double reflections (a weak reflection from the surface of the glass, and a stronger one from the reflecting metal) and reduces absorption of light by the mirror. Technical mirrors may use a silver, aluminium, or gold coating (the latter typically for infrared mirrors), and achieve reflectivities of 90-95 per cent when new. A protective transparent overcoat may be applied to prevent oxidation of the reflective layer. Applications requiring higher reflectivity or greater durability where wide bandwidth is not essential use dielectric coatings, which can achieve reflectivities as high as 99.999 per cent over a narrow range of wavelengths.

There are many types of glass mirrors, each of them representing a different manufacturing process and reflection type.

An aluminum glass mirror is made of a float glass manufactured using vacuum coating, i.e. aluminum is spread over the glass in the vacuum chamber and then coated with two or more layers of waterproof protective paint. Aluminum glass mirror provides an actual and accurate reflection.

Silver Glass Mirror is an ordinary mirror coated on its back surface with silver that produces images by reflection. This kind of glass mirror is produced by coating a silver, copper film and two or more layers of waterproof paint on the back surface of float glass, which perfectly resists acid and moisture. Silver glass mirror provides clear and actual images, is quite durable and is widely used for furniture, bathroom and other decoration purposes.

Low Aluminum Glass Mirror is manufactured by coating silver and two layers of protective paint on the back surface of glass. Low aluminum glass mirror is very clear, light transmissive, smooth, and reflects accurate natural colours. This type of glass is widely used for framing presentations and exhibitions in which a precise colour representation of the artwork is truly essential or when the background colour of the frame is predominantly white.

Safety Glass Mirror is made of a glass silver mirror by sticking a special protective film in the back surface of the mirror, which prevents injuries in case the mirror is broken. This kind of mirror is used for furniture, doors, glass walls, commercial shelves, or public areas.

Silkscreen Printed Glass Mirror is produced using inorganic colour ink that prints patterns through a special screen onto glass. Various colours, patterns, and glass shapes are available. Such glass mirror is durable and more moisture resistant than an ordinary printed glass and can server for over 20 years. This type of glass is widely used for decoration purposes (mirrors, table tops, doors, windows, kitchen chop boards, etc.)

Decorative Glass Mirrors are usually handcrafted. Different shades, shapes and glass thickness are often available.

Effects

In a plane mirror, a parallel beam of light changes its direction as a whole, while still remaining parallel; the images formed by a plane mirror are virtual images, of the same size as the original object. There are also concave mirrors, where a parallel beam of light becomes a convergent beam, whose rays intersect in the focus of the mirror. Lastly, there are convex mirrors, where a parallel beam becomes divergent, with the rays appearing to diverge from a common intersection 'behind' the mirror. Spherical concave and convex mirrors do not focus parallel rays to a single point due to spherical aberration. However, the ideal of focussing to a point is a commonly-used approximation. Parabolic reflectors resolve this, allowing incoming parallel rays (for example, light from a distant star) to be focussed to a small spot; almost an ideal point. Parabolic reflectors are not suitable for imaging nearby objects because the light rays are not parallel.

A beam of light reflects off a mirror at an angle of reflection that is equal to its angle of incidence (if the size of a mirror is much larger than the wavelength of light). That is, if the beam of light is shining on a mirror's surface at a 30° angle from vertical, then it reflects from the point of incidence at a 30° angle from vertical in the opposite direction.

Safety and Easier Viewing

Rear-view mirrors are widely used in and on vehicles (such as automobiles, or bicycles), to allow drivers to see other vehicles coming up behind them. Some motorcycle helmets have a built-in so-called MROS (Multiple Reflective Optic System): a set of reflective surfaces inside the helmet that together function as a rear-view mirror. There exist rear view sunglasses, of which the left end of the left glass and the right end of the right glass work as mirrors.

Convex mirrors are used to provide a wider field of view than a flat mirror, and are often used on vehicles, especially large trucks, to minimise blind spots. They are sometimes placed at road junctions, and corners of places such as parking lots to allow people to see around corners to avoid crashing into other vehicles or shopping carts. They are also sometimes used as part of security systems, so that a single video camera can show more than one angle at a time.

Mouth mirrors or 'dental mirrors' are used by dentists to allow indirect vision and lighting within the mouth. Their reflective surfaces may be either flat or curved. Mouth mirrors are also commonly used by engineers to allow vision in tight spaces and around corners in equipment.

A *two-way mirror* is a sheet of glass coated with a layer of metal only a few dozen atoms thick, which reflects some percentage of the light incident on it and transmits the remainder to the other side.

It is typically used as an apparently normal mirror in a brightly lit room, with a much darker room on the other side. People on the brightly lit side see their own reflection — it looks like a normal mirror. People on the dark side see through it — it looks like a transparent window. The light from the bright room reflected from the mirror back into the room itself is much greater than the light transmitted from the dark room, overwhelming the small amount of light transmitted from the dark to the bright room; conversely, the light reflected back into the dark side is overwhelmed by the light transmitted from the bright side. This allows a viewer in the dark side to observe the bright room covertly.

The reality television programme Big Brother makes extensive use of two-way mirrors throughout its set to allow cameramen in special black hallways to use movable cameras to film contestants without being seen.

The same type of mirror, when used in an optical instrument, is called a *half-silvered mirror* or beam splitter. Its purpose is quite different: to split a beam of light so that part, usually about half, passes straight through, while the other part is reflected. In a typical scientific application the two resulting beams are made to interfere after traversing different paths. An unusual single-lens reflex camera used a half-silvered mirror to create an image of the scene both in the film plane and in the viewfinder.

One-way mirrors work by overwhelming dim transmitted light with bright reflected light. A true one-way mirror that actually allows light to be transmitted in one direction only without requiring external energy is not possible as it violates the second law of thermodynamics: if we place a cold object on the transmitting side and a hot one on the blocked side, radiant energy would be transferred from the cold to the hot object.

One-way windows can be made to work with polarized light in the laboratory without violating the second law. This is an apparent paradox that stumped some great physicists, although it does not allow a practical one-way mirror for use in the real world. Optical isolators are one-way devices that are commonly used with lasers.

With the sun as light source, a mirror can be used to signal by variations in the orientation of the mirror. The signal can be used over long distances, possibly up to 60 kilometres on a clear day. This technique was used by Native American tribes and numerous militaries to transmit information between distant outposts.

Mirrors can also be used for rescue, especially to attract the attention of search and rescue helicopters. Specialised signalling mirrors are available and are often included in military survival kits.

Technology

Televisions and Projectors

Microscopic mirrors are a core element of many of the largest high-definition televisions and video projectors. A common technology of this type is Texas Instruments' DLP. A DLP chip is a postage stamp-sized microchip whose surface is an array of millions of microscopic mirrors. The picture is created as the individual mirrors move to either reflect light toward the projection surface (pixel on), or toward a light absorbing surface (pixel off).

Other projection technologies involving mirrors include LCoS. Like a DLP chip, LCoS is a microchip of similar size, but rather than millions of individual mirrors, there is a single mirror that is actively shielded by a liquid crystal matrix with up to millions of pixels. The picture is formed as light is either reflected toward the projection surface (pixel on), or absorbed by the activated LCD pixels (pixel off). LCoS-based televisions and projectors often use 3 chips, one for each primary colour.

Large mirrors are used in rear projection televisions. Light (for example from a DLP as mentioned above) is 'folded' by one or more mirrors so that the television set is compact.

Instruments

Telescopes and other precision instruments use *front silvered* or first surface mirrors, where the reflecting surface is placed on the front (or first) surface of the glass (this eliminates reflection from glass surface ordinary back mirrors have). Some of them use silver, but most are aluminum, which is more reflective at short wavelengths than silver. All of these coatings are easily damaged and require special handling. They reflect 90 per cent to 95 per cent of the incident light when new. The coatings are typically applied by vacuum deposition. A protective overcoat is usually applied before the mirror is removed from the vacuum, because the coating otherwise begins to corrode as soon as it is exposed to oxygen and humidity in the air. *Front silvered* mirrors have to be resurfaced occasionally to keep their quality. There are optical mirrors such as mangin mirrors that are *second surface mirrors* (reflective coating on the rear surface) as part of their optical designs, usually to correct optical aberrations.

The reflectivity of the mirror coating can be measured using a reflectometer and for a particular metal it will be different for different wavelengths of light. This is exploited in some optical work to make cold mirrors and hot mirrors. A cold mirror is made by using a transparent substrate and choosing a coating material that is more reflective to visible light and more transmissive to infrared light. A hot mirror is the opposite, the coating preferentially reflects infrared. Mirror surfaces are sometimes given thin film overcoatings both to retard degradation of the surface and to increase their reflectivity in parts of the spectrum where they will be used. For instance, aluminum mirrors are commonly coated with silicon dioxide or magnesium fluoride. The reflectivity as a function of wavelength depends on both the thickness of the coating and on how it is applied.

A dielectric coated mirror used in a dye laser. The mirror is over 99 per cent reflective at 550 nanometers, (yellow), but will allow most other colours to pass through.

For scientific optical work, dielectric mirrors are often used. These are glass (or sometimes other material) substrates on which one or more layers of dielectric material are deposited, to form an optical coating. By careful choice of the type and thickness of the dielectric layers, the range of wavelengths and amount of light reflected from the mirror can be specified. The best mirrors of this type can reflect >99.999 per cent of the light (in a narrow range of wavelengths) which is incident on the mirror. Such mirrors are often used in lasers.

In astronomy, adaptive optics is a technique to measure variable image distortions and adapt a deformable mirror accordingly on a timescale of milliseconds, to compensate for the distortions.

Although the most of mirrors are designed to reflect visible light, surfaces reflecting other forms of electro-magnetic radiation are also called 'mirrors'. The mirrors for other ranges of electromagnetic waves are used in optics and astronomy. Mirrors for radio waves are important elements of radio telescopes.

Face-to-face Mirrors

A dielectric mirror used in lasers.

Two or more mirrors placed exactly face to face give the appearance of an infinite regress. Some devices use this to generate multiple reflections:

- Fabry-Pérot interferometer.
- Laser (which contains an optical cavity).
- Some types of catoptric cistula.
- Momentum-enhanced solar sail.

It has been said that Archimedes used a large array of mirrors to burn Roman ships during an attack on Syracuse. This has never been proven or disproved; however, it has been put to the test. Recently, on a popular Discovery Channel show, MythBusters, a team from MIT tried to recreate the famous 'Archimedes Death Ray'. They were successful at starting a fire on a ship at 75 feet away; however, previous attempts to light the boat on fire using only the bronze mirrors available in Archimedes' time were unsuccessful, and the time taken to ignite the craft would have made its use impractical, resulting in the MythBusters team deeming the myth 'busted'.

Seasonal Lighting

Due to its location in a steep-sided valley, the Italian town of Viganella gets no direct sunlight for seven weeks each winter. In 2006 a · 100,000 computer-controlled mirror, 8 × 5 m, was installed to reflect sunlight into the town's piazza. In early 2007 the similarly situated village of Bondo, Switzerland, was considering applying this solution as well. Mirrors can be used to produce enhanced lighting effects in greenhouses or conservatories.

Leisure

Decoration

Mirrors, typically large and unframed, are frequently used in interior decoration to create an illusion of space, and amplify the apparent size of a room.

Mirrors are used also in some schools of feng shui, an ancient Chinese practice of placement and arrangement of space to achieve harmony with the environment.

The softness of old mirrors is sometimes replicated by contemporary artisans for use in interior design. These reproduction antiqued mirrors are works of art and can bring colour and texture to an otherwise hard, cold reflective surface. It is an artistic process that has been attempted by many and perfected by few.

Entertainment

The hall of mirrors, commonly found in amusement parks, is an attraction in which a number of distorted mirrors are used to produce unusual reflections of the visitor. Mirror mazes, also found in amusement parks, contain large numbers of mirrors and sheets of glass. The idea is to navigate the disorientating array without bumping into the walls. Mirrors in attractions like this are often made of plexiglass as to assure that they do not break.

Mirrors are often used in magic to create an illusion. One effect is called Pepper's ghost. Illuminated rotating disco balls covered with small mirrors are used to cast moving spots of light around a dance floor. Mirrors are employed in kaleidoscopes, personal entertainment devices invented in Scotland by sir David Brewster.

Art

Filippo Brunelleschi discovered linear perspective with the help of the mirror, Leonardo da Vinci called the mirror the 'master of painters'. He recommended, "When you wish to see whether your whole picture accords with what you have portrayed from nature take a mirror and reflect the actual object in it. Compare what is reflected with your painting and carefully consider whether both likenesses of the subject correspond, particularly in regard to the mirror." The mirror is the central device in some of the greatest of European paintings: Jan Van Eyck's Arnolfini Portrait, Titian's *Venus with a mirror*, Veronese's *Venus with a mirror*, Diego Velazquez's Las Meninas and Edouard Manet's A Bar at the Folies-Bergère. Without a mirror, the great self portraits by Dürer, Rembrandt, Van Gogh and Frida Kahlo could not have been painted. M.C. Escher used special shapes of mirrors in order to have a much more complete view of the surroundings than by direct observation (Hand with Reflecting Sphere). István Orosz's anamorphic works are images distorted such way that they only become clearly visible when reflected in a suitably-shaped and positioned mirror. Some other contemporary artists use mirrors as the material of art, like in mirror-sculptures and paintings on mirror surfaces. Some artists build special mirror installations as the neon mirror cubes by Jeppe Hein.

Painters depicting someone gazing into a mirror often also show the person's reflection. This is a kind of abstraction — in most cases the angle of view is such that the person's reflection should not be visible. Similarly, in movies and still photography an actor or actress is often shown ostensibly looking at him or herself in the mirror, and yet the reflection faces the camera. In reality, the actor or actress sees only the camera and its operator in this case, not their own reflection.

Literature

Mirrors play a powerful role in cultural literature, from the self-loving Narcissus of Greek Mythology to the Biblical reference to Through a Glass Darkly. In the European fairy-tale Snow White, the evil queen asked, "Mirror, mirror, on the wall . . . who's the fairest of them all?" Some of the best-loved uses of mirrors in literature include Lewis Carroll's Through the Looking Glass and the Mirror of Erised in the Harry Potter series. Horror movies about mirrors include Candyman and Mirrors.

Mirrors and Superstition

There are many legends and superstitions surrounding mirrors. Mirrors are said to be a reflection of the soul, and they were often used in traditional witchcraft as tools for scrying or performing other spells. It is also said that mirrors cannot lie. They can show only the truth, so it is a very bad omen indeed to see something in a mirror which should not be there. Also there is a legend that a newborn child should not see a mirror until its first birthday as its soul is still developing. If the child sees its reflection it is said that it will die.

It is a common superstition that someone who breaks a mirror will receive seven years of bad luck. One of the many reasons for this belief is that the mirror is believed to reflect part of the soul, therefore, breaking the mirror will break part of the soul. However, the soul is said to regenerate every seven years, thus coming back unbroken. To counter this one of many rituals has to be performed, the easiest of which is to stop the mirror from reflecting the broken soul by grinding it to dust. The belief might also simply originate from the high cost of mirrors in times gone past. It is also said that tapping the broken mirror on a gravestone seven times will allow the soul to heal. Another option is to bury the mirror, also preventing the mirror from reflecting the broken soul. However, if the mirror is both touched to the gravestone and buried, the bad luck will remain. If you are in this position, the only course of action is to dig up the mirror and grind it to dust. Finally, this dust must be sprinkled around the same gravestone on which the mirror was initially tapped.

In days past it was customary in the southern United States to cover the mirrors in a house where the wake of a deceased person was being held. It was believed that the person's soul would become trapped in a mirror left uncovered. This practice is still followed in other countries (Greece), extending to everything that could reflect the deceased person's face (like TV appliances); another explanation given is that the devil will appear in the reflection of the dead. Mirrors falling from walls or otherwise breaking or cracking mysteriously were said to be haunted.

According to legend, a vampire has no reflection in mirrors because it is an undead creature and has already lost its soul.

Other types of reflecting device are also called 'mirrors'. For example metallic reflectors are used to reflect infrared light (such as in space heaters), or microwaves.

An acoustic mirror is a passive device used to reflect and perhaps to focus sound waves. Acoustic mirrors were used for selective detection of sound waves, especially during World War II. They were used for detection of enemy aircraft prior to the development of radar. Acoustic mirrors are used for remote probing of the atmosphere; they can be used to form a narrow diffraction-limited beam. They can also be used for underwater imaging.

Active mirrors are mirrors that amplify the light they reflect. They are used to make disk lasers. The amplification is typically over a narrow range of wavelengths, and requires an external source of power.

An atomic mirror is a device which reflects matter waves. Usually, atomic mirrors work at grazing incidence. Such a mirror can be used for atomic interferometry and atomic holography. It has been proposed that they can be used for non-destructive imaging systems with nanometer resolution.

Cold mirrors are dielectric mirrors that reflect the entire visible light spectrum while efficiently transmitting infrared wavelengths. Conversely, hot mirrors reflect infrared light while allowing visible light to pass. These can be used to separate useful light from unneeded infrared to reduce heating of components in an optical device. They can also be used as dichroic beamsplitters.

Corner reflectors use three flat mirrors to reflect light back towards its source. They are used for emergency location, and even laser ranging to the Moon.

X-ray mirrors produce specular reflection of X-rays. All known types work only at angles near grazing incidence, and only a small fraction of the rays are reflected.

A non-reversing mirror is a mirror that provides a non-reversed image of its subject.

13

Studio Glass

Studio glass or *glass sculpture* is the modern use of glass as an artistic medium to produce sculptures or two-dimensional artworks. Specific approaches include working glass at room temperature cold working, stained glass, working glass in a torch flame (lampworking), glass beadmaking, glass casting, glass fusing, and, most notably, glass blowing. As a decorative and functional medium, glass was extensively developed in Egypt and Assyria, brought to the fore by the Romans (who spread glassblowing, invented by the Phoenicians), and includes among its greatest triumphs European cathedral stained glass windows. Great ateliers like Tiffany, Lalique, Daum, Gallé, the Corning schools in upper New York state, and Steuben Glass Works took glass art to the highest levels. Glass from Murano (also known as Venetian glass) is the result of hundreds of years of refinement and invention. Murano is still held as the birthplace of modern glass art.

The glass objects created are intended to make a sculptural or decorative statement. On the market, their prices may range from a few hundred to tens of thousands of dollars (US).

Before about the early 1960s, contemporary glass art had mostly been glass made for decorative use, usually by teams of factory workers, taking glass from furnaces with a thousand or more pounds of glass. This form of glass art, of which Tiffany and Steuben in the U.S.A., Gallé in France and Hoya Crystal in Japan, Royal Leerdam Crystal in The Netherlands and Orrefors and Kosta Boda in Sweden are perhaps the best known, grew out of the factory system in which all glass objects were hand or mold blown by teams of 4 or more men. The turn of the 19th Century was the height of the old art glass movement while the factory glass blowers were being replaced by mechanical bottle blowing and continuous window glass.

The United States has had two phases of development in glass. The early and mid-1900s had a number of factories active in Ohio and Corning, NY. with factories such as Fenton, Steuben and others turning out both functional and artistic pieces. The second phase of glass in the United States happened in the 60's as Harvey Littleton, Dominick Labino and Marvin Lipofsky kicked off the studio glass movement by creating small-scale furnaces for the use of glass as an artisic medium. This modern studio glass movement caught on in design schools and Littleton would go on to found the first fine art glass programme at the University of Wisconsin–Madison; Marvin Lipofsky, founded the university-level glass programme at the University of California at Berkeley in 1964. Dr. Robert C. Fritz founded a university-level glass programme at San Jose State University in San Jose, CA the same semester in 1964. In 1965 Bill H. Boysen, as a graduate student under Harvey Littleton, built the first glass studio at Penland School of Crafts, Penland, North Carolina. After graduating from the University of Wisconsin–Madison in 1966, Boysen started the graduate glass programme at Southern Illinois University at Carbondale, Illinois later that same year. Dale Chihuly initiated the glass programme at the Rhode Island School of Design in 1969.

As glass grew in the U.S. and artists learned from artists before them there has been a growth of studio art glass distributed across the country, but with the largest concentration of glass artists working in Seattle, New York, Pennsylvania and New Jersey. San Francisco, Los Angeles/ Orange County and Corning also have sizable concentrations of artists working in glass. The Pilchuck Glass School near Seattle has become a mecca for glass artists from all over the world. Students, who may actually be college students or established artists, have the opportunity to attend master classes and exchange skills and information in an environment dedicated solely to glass based arts. The Pittsburgh Glass Center in Pittsburgh Pa. has residency programmes for artists working in glass, as well as a facility for artists to make use of for their works. The Pittsburgh Glass Centre offers classes to the public on glassblowing and many other forms of glass art. Philadelphia hosts a small array of glass studios for artists that use glass. Home to the National Liberty Museum (featuring all exhibits by international glass artists), Philadelphia hosts the non-profit P.I.P.E programme, with residencies for artists that use glass as well as metal, electroforming on glass, and bronze casting. The state of Pennsylvania has a long tradition of the production of industrial glass and its influence has quickly been absorbed by artists working in glass. Wheaton Arts and Cultural Centre located in New Jersey, just below Glassboro, is a non-profit that hosts a fellowship programme exclusively for artists working in glass.

Italy

Glass blowing began in the Roman Empire, and Italy has refined the techniques of glass blowing ever since. Until the very recent explosion of glass shops in Seattle (USA), there were more on the Island of Murano (Italy) than anywhere else in world. The majority of the refined artistic techniques of glassblowing (e.g., incalmo, reticello, zanfirico, latticino) were developed there. Moreover, generations of blowers passed on their techniques to family members. Boys would begin working at the *fornazi* (actually 'furnace'— called 'the factory' in English).

United Kingdom

Glass sculpture by Dale Chihuly at a 2005 exhibition in Kew Gardens, London, England. The piece is 13 feet (4 m) high.

Notable centres of glass production in the UK have been St. Helens in Merseyside (the home of Pilkington Glass and the site on which lead crystal glass was first produced by George Ravenscroft), Stourbridge in the Midlands and Sunderland in the North East. Sunderland is now home to The National Glass Centre which houses a specialist glass art course. St. Helens boasts a similar establishment but without the educational body attached. Perthshire in Scotland was known internationally for its glass paperweights. It has always hosted the best glass artists working on small scales, but closed its factory in Crieff, Scotland in January 2002.

Glass artists in the UK have a variety of exhibitions. The Scottish Glass Society hosts a yearly exhibition for members, the Guild of Glass Engravers exhibit every two years and the British Glass Biennale, begun in 2004 is now opening its third show.

British Glass Art owes much to the long history of craft. The majority of its glass blowers who operate small studio furnaces produce aesthetically beautiful though primarily functional objects. Technical skill as a blower is given as much importance as the artistic intent. Other notable Glasshouse artists are Steven Newell, Catherine Hough, Annette Meech and of course Simon Moore.

There are a growing number of art glass studios in the UK. Many specialize in production glassware while others concentrate on one off or limited edition pieces. An Arts Council funded, non-profit making organisation, the Contemporary Glass Society, founded in 1976 as *British Artists in Glass*, exists to promote and support the work of glass artists in the UK.

Other glass organisations in the UK are The Guild of Glass Engravers, the Scottish Glass Society and Cohesion. Cohesion is a different sort of entity to the other organisations in that it was specifically founded to promote and develop glass art as a commercial concern. It organises trade events in and around the UK and at the international level. Originally it focussed only on artists based the north east of England but has since expanded its remit to cover the whole of the UK.

The Northlands Glass School was established in late 1990s in the far north of Scotland and offers residencies and masterclasses to arts students and established glass artists.

In November 2007 the glass sculpture *Model for a Hotel* was unveiled as an exhibit on the fourth plinth of Trafalgar Square, London.

China

In China, the making of glass arts date back to the Western Han Dynastry of the 3rd century BC. 'Liuli' is the name of an ancient form of Chinese glassmaking. Today, Liuli Gongfang is Taiwan's only contemporary glass studio devoted to artistic Chinese glassware.

Japan

Japanese glass art has a short history. The first independent glass studios were built by Saburo Funakoshi and Makoto Ito, and Shinzo Kotani in separate places. Yoshihiko Takahashi and Hiroshi Yamano show their works at galleries throughout the world and are arguably Japan's glass artists of note. Yoichi Ohira has worked with great success in Murano with Italian gaffers. The small Pacific island Niijima, administered by Tokyo. has a renowned glass art centre, built and run by Osamu and Yumiko Noda, graduates of Illinois State University, where they studied with Joel Philip Myers. Every autumn, the Niijima International Glass Art Festival takes place inviting top international glass artists for demonstrations and seminars. Emerging glass artists, such as Yukako Kojima and Tomoe Shizumu, were featured at the 2007 Glass Art Society exhibition space at the Pittsburgh Glass Centre. Kyohei Fujita was another noteworthy Japanese studio glass artist.

Australia

The early glass movement (studio glass) in Australia was spurred on by a visit to Australia by American artist Richard Marquis, who toured the country in the early seventies with a mobile studio assisted by Australian Nick Mount. Since that time Australian glass has gained worldwide recognition with Adelaide in South Australia, hosting the International Glass Art Society Conference in 2005 on only its third occasion outside of the U.S.A.

Mexico

Mexico was the first country in Latin America to have a glass factory in the early sixteenth century brought by the Spanish conquerors. Although traditional glass in Mexico has prevailed over modern glass art, since the 1970s there have been glass artists that have given a place to that country in international glass art.

The Netherlands

Glass art in the Netherlands is mainly stimulated by the glass designing and glass blowing factory Royal Leerdam Crystal. Such notable designers as H.P. Berlage, Andries Copier and Willem Heesen (Master Glassblower as well) had a major influence on Dutch glass art. Later the studio glass movement, inspired by the American Harvey Littleton and the new Masterstudy Glass art at the Gerrit Rietveld Academy in Amsterdam led to a new generation of glass artists.

Belgium

In Leuven lain near Brussels are themselves the glass factory of Belgian glass styling Theys & Miseur which represent Belgian artistic glass work concerning the entire world. Here works the master glass-makers Daniël Theys , Chris Miseur and their son Daan Theys. These masters are unique in what they make. Daan Theys combines glass-blowing with his artistic career of contemporary art. The studio is well known all over the world for making high-quality glass art.

The international studio glass movement originated in America, spreading to Europe, the United Kingdom, Australia and Asia. The emphasis of this movement was on the artist as the designer and maker of one-of-a-kind objects. This movement enabled the sharing of technical knowledge and ideas among artists and designers that, in industry, would not be possible.

With the dominance of Modernism in the arts, there was a broadening of artistic media throughout the 20th century. Indeed, glass was part of the curriculum at art schools such as the Bauhaus. Frank Lloyd Wright's produced glass windows considered by some as masterpieces not only of design, but of painterly composition as well. During the 1950s, studio ceramics and other craft media in the U.S. began to gain in popularity and importance, and American artists interested in glass looked for new paths outside industry. Harvey Littleton, often referred to as the "Father of the Studio Glass Movement", was inspired to develop studio glassblowing in America by the great glass being designed and made in Italy, Sweden and many other places, and by the pioneering work in ceramics of the California potter Peter Voulkos. Together with Dominic Labino, Littleton staged a now-famous glass workshop at the Toledo Museum of Art in 1962.

Creating Art made from Glass

There are many ways to create and decorate a piece of art from glass. Blown glass, where a glassblower works at a furnace full of molten glass using metal rods and hand tools to blow and shape almost any form of glass, is one of the older and more popular ways to work. Most large hollow pieces are made this way, and it allows the artist to be improvisational as they create their work as it is very hands on.

Another type is flame-worked glass, which uses torches and kilns in its production. The artist generally works at a bench using rods and tubes of glass, shaping with hand tools to create their work. Many forms can be achieved this way with little investment into money and space. Though the artist is somewhat limited in size, a greater level of detail can be achieved with this technique. Paul Stankard's art is a good example of the level of detail that can be done with flameworking techniques.

Cast glass can be done at the furnace at the torch or in a kiln. generally the artist makes a mold out of refractory, sand, or plaster and silica which can be filled with either clear glass or coloured or patterned glass, depending on the techniques and effects desired. Large scale sculpture is usually created this way.

Slumped glass and fused glass is similar to cast glass, but it is not done at as high of a temperature. Usually the glass is only heated enough to impress a shape or a texture onto the piece, or to stick several pieces of glass together without a glue.

With stained glass the artist cuts the glass into specific patterns to make their artwork which are stuck together using lead came and solder. They can also use hot techniques in a kiln to create texture, patterns, or change the overall shape of the glass.

Etched glass is created by dipping glass that has an acid resistant pattern applied to its surface into an acid solution. Also an artist can engrave it by hand using wheels. Sandblasting can create a similar effect.

14

Glassblowing

As a novel glass forming technique created in the middle of the last century B.C., glassblowing exploited a working property of glass which was previously unknown to the glassworkers — inflation. Inflation refers to the expansion of a molten blob of glass by introducing a small amount of air to it. This property is based on the liquid structure of glass where the atoms are held together by strong chemical bonds in a disordered and random network, therefore molten glass is viscous enough to be blown and gradually hardens as it loses heat. In order to increase the stiffness of the molten glass, which in turn facilitates the process of blowing, there is a subtle change in the composition of glass. With reference to their studies of the ancient glass assemblages from Sepphoris of Israel, Fischer and McCray postulated that the concentration of natron, which acts as flux in glass, is slightly lower in blown vessels than those manufactured by casting. Lower concentration of natron would have allowed the glass to be stiffer for blowing. A full range of glassblowing techniques was developed within decades of its invention and the two major methods of glassblowing are as follows:

Free-blowing

This method held a pre-eminent position in glassforming ever since its introduction in the middle of the first century B.C. until the late nineteenth century and is still widely used nowadays as a glassforming technique. The process of free-blowing involves the blowing of short puffs of air into a molten portion of glass which is gathered at one end of the blowpipe. This has the effect of forming an elastic skin on the interior of the glass blob that matches the exterior caused by the removal of heat from the furnace. The glassworker can then quickly inflate the molten glass to a coherent blob and work it into a desired shape. The Toledo Museum of Art attempted to reconstruct the ancient free-blowing technique by using clay blowpipes. The result proved that short clay blowpipes of about 30-60 cm facilitate free-blowing because they are simple to handle, easy to manipulate and can be re-used several times. Skilled workers are capable of shaping almost any vessel forms by rotating the pipe, swinging it and controlling the temperature of the piece while they blow. They can produce a great variety of glass objects, ranging from drinking cups to window glass.

An outstanding example of the free-blowing technique is the Portland Vase which is a cameo manufactured during the Roman period. An experiment was carried out by Gudenrath and Whitehouse with the aim of re-creating the Portland Vase. A full amount of blue glass required for the body of the vase was gathered on the end of the blowpipe and was subsequently dipped into a pot of hot white glass. Inflation occurred when the glassworker blew the molten glass into a sphere which was then stretched or elongated into a vase with a layer of white glass overlying the blue body.

In Modern Context

The transformation of raw materials into glass takes place around 2400 °F (1315 °C); the glass emits enough heat to appear almost white hot. The glass is then left to 'fine out' (allowing the bubbles to rise out of the mass), and then the working temperature is reduced in the furnace to around 2000 °F (1100°C). At this stage, the glass appears to be a bright orange colour. Though most glassblowing is done between 1600-1900°F (870-1040°C), 'Soda-lime' glass remains somewhat plastic and workable as low as 1350 °F (730°C). Annealing is usually done between 800-900°F (430-480 °C).

Glassblowing involves three furnaces. The first, which contains a crucible of molten glass, is simply referred to as 'the furnace'. The second is called the 'glory hole', and is used to reheat a piece in between steps of working with it. The final furnace is called the 'lehr' or 'annealer', and is used to slowly cool the glass, over a period of a few hours to a few days, depending on the size of the pieces. This keeps the glass from cracking due to thermal stress. Historically, all three furnaces were contained in one, with a set of progressively cooler chambers for each of the three purposes. Many glassblowing studios in Mexico and South America still employ this method.

The major tools involved are the blowpipe (or blow tube), the punty, bench, marver, seers, blocks, jacks, paddles, tweezers, and a variety of shears. The tip of the blowpipe is first preheated; then dipped in the molten glass in the furnace. The molten glass is 'gathered' on to the blowpipe in much the same way that honey is picked up on a dipper.

Then, this glass is rolled on the marver , which was traditionally a flat slab of marble, but today is more commonly a fairly thick flat sheet of steel. This forms a cool skin on the exterior of the molten glass and shapes it. Then air is blown into the pipe, creating a bubble. Then, one can gather over that bubble to create a larger piece. Blocks are ladle-like tools made from water-soaked fruit wood and are used similarly to the marver to shape and cool a piece in the early steps of creation. The bench is a glassblower's workstation, and has a place for the glassblower to sit, a place for the handheld tools, and two rails that the pipe or punty rides on while the blower works with the piece. Jacks are a tool shaped somewhat like large tweezers with two blades. Jacks are used for forming shape later in the creation of a piece. Paddles are flat pieces of wood or graphite used for creating flat spots like a bottom. Tweezers are used to pick out details or to pull on the glass. There are two important types of shears, straight shears and diamond shears. Straight shears are essentially bulky scissors, used for making linear cuts. Diamond shears have blades that form a diamond shape when partially open. These are used for cutting off masses of glass. Once a piece has been blown to its approximate final size, the bottom is finalized. Then, the piece is transferred to a punty, and the top is finalized. There are many ways to apply patterns and colour to blown glass, including rolling molten glass in powdered colour or larger pieces of coloured glass called frit.

Complex patterns with great detail can be created through the use of cane (rods of coloured glass) and murrine (rods cut in cross-sections to reveal patterns). These pieces of colour can be arranged in a pattern and 'picked up' by rolling a bubble of molten glass over them. One of the most exacting and complicated caneworking techniques is 'reticello', which involves creating two bubbles from cane, each twisted in a different direction and then combining them and blowing out the final form.

A lampworker, usually operating on a much smaller scale, historically used alcohol lamps and breath or bellows-driven air to create a hot flame at a workbench to manipulate preformed glass rods and tubes. These stock materials took form as laboratory glass, beads, and durable scientific 'specimens' — miniature glass sculpture. The craft, which was raised to an art form in the late 1960s by Hans Godo Frabel (later followed by lampwork artists such as Milon Townsend and Robert Mickelson), is still practised today. The modern lampworker uses a flame of oxygen and propane or natural gas. The modern torch permits working both the soft glass from the furnace worker and the borosilicate glass (low-expansion) of the scientific glassblower who may have multiple headed torches and special lathes to help form the glass or fused quartz used for special projects. The molten glass is attached to a stainless steel or iron rod called a punty (or a punty rod, a pontil, or a mandrel) for shaping and transferring a hollow piece from the blowpipe for an opening to create from.

History

Origins

Glassblowing is a glass forming technique which was invented by the Phoenicians at approximately 50 B.C. somewhere along the Syro-Palestinian coast. The earliest evidence of glassblowing comes from a collection of waste from a glass workshop, including fragments of glass tubes, glass rods and tiny blown bottles, which was dumped in a mikvah, a ritual bath in the Jewish Quarter of Old City of Jerusalem dated from 37 to 4 B.C. Some of the glass tubes recovered are fire-closed at one end and are partially inflated by blowing through the open end while still hot to form small bottle, thus they are considered as a rudimentary form of blowpipe. Hence, tube blowing not only represents the initial attempts of experimentation by glassworkers at blowing glass, it is also a revolutionary step the induced a change in conception and a deep understanding of glass. Such invention swiftly eclipsed all other traditional methods, such as casting and core-forming, in working glass.

The invention of glassblowing was coincided with the establishment of the Roman Empire in the first century B.C. which served to provide impetus to its spread and dominance. Glassblowing was greatly encouraged under the Roman rule, although Roman citizens could not be 'in trade', in particular under the reign of Augustus, therefore glass was being blown in many areas of the Roman world. On the eastern borders of the Empire, the first glass workshops were set up by the Phoenicians in the birthplace of glassblowing in contemporary Syria, Israel, and Palestine, as well as in the neighbouring province of Cyprus. Ennion for example, was among one of the most prominent glassworkers from Syria of the time. He was renowned for producing the multi-paneled mould-blown glass vessels that were complex in their shapes, arrangement and decorative motifs. The complexity of designs of these mould-blown glass vessels illustrated that the sophistication of the glassworkers in the eastern regions of the Roman Empire. Mould-blown glass vessels manufactured by the workshops of Ennion and other contemporary glassworkers such as Jason, Nikon, Aristeas and Meges, constitutes some of the earliest evidence of glassblowing found in the eastern territories. Meanwhile, the glassblowing technique reached Egypt and was described in a fragmentary poem printed on the papyrus which was dated to third century A.D. Besides, the Roman hegemony over the Mediterranean areas resulted in the substitution of Hellenistic casting, core-forming and mosaic fusion techniques by blowing. The earliest evidence of blowing in Hellenistic consists of small blown bottles for perfume and oil retrieved from the glass workshops on the Greek island of Samothrace and at Corinth in mainland Greece which were dated to first century A.D.

On the other hand, the Phoenician glassworkers exploited their glassblowing techniques and set up their workshops in the western territories of the Roman Empire first in Italy by the middle of the first century A.D. Rome, the heartland of the Empire, soon became a major glassblowing centre and more glassblowing workshops were subsequently established in other provinces of Italy, for example Campania, Morgantina and Aquileia. A great variety of blown glass objects, ranging from unguentaria (toiletry container for perfume) to cameo, from tableware to window glass, were produced. From there, escaping craftsmen forbidden to travel otherwise advanced to the rest of Europe by building their glassblowing workshops in the north of the Alps which is now Switzerland and then at sites in northern Europe in present-day France and Belgium. Surviving evidence, such as blowpipes and moulds which are indicative of the presence of blowing, was fragmentary and limited. Fragments of clay blowpipes were retrieved from the late first century A.D. glass workshop at Avenches in Switzerland. Clay blowpipes, also known as mouthblowers, were made by the ancient glassworkers due to the accessibility and availability of the resources before the introduction of the metal blowpipes. Hollow iron rods, together with blown vessel fragments and glass waste dating to approximately fourth century A.D, were recovered from the glass workshop in Merida of Spain, as well as in Salona in Croatia. Meanwhile, one of the most prolific glassblowing centres of the Roman period was established in Cologne on the river Rhine in Germany by late first century B.C. Stone base mould and terracotta base mould were discovered from these Rhineland workshops suggesting the adoption and the application of mould-blowing technique by the glassworkers. Besides, blown flagons and blown jars decorated with ribbing, as well as blown perfume bottles with letters CCAA or CCA which stand for Colonia Claudia Agrippiniensis, were produced from the Rhineland workshops. Remains of blown blue-green glass vessels, for example bottles with a handle, collared bowls and indented beakers, were found in abundance from the local glass workshops at Poetovio and Celeia in Slovenia.

The glassblowing tradition was carried on in Europe from the mediaeval period through the Middle Ages to the Renaissance in the demise of the Roman Empire in the fifth century A.D. During the early mediaeval period, the Franks manipulated the technique of glassblowing by creating the simple corrugated moulds and developing the claws decoration techniques. Blown glass objects, such as the drinking vessels that imitated the shape of the animal horn were produced in the Rhine and Meuse valleys, as well as in Belgium. On the other hand, the Renaissance Europe witnessed the revitalization of glass industry in Italy. Glassblowing, in particular the mould-blowing technique, was employed by the Venetian glassworkers from Murano to produce the fine glassware which is also known as cristallo. The technique of glassblowing, coupled with the cylinder and crown methods, was used to manufacture sheet or flat glass for window panes in the late seventeenth century. The applicability of glassblowing was so widespread that glass was being blown in many parts of the world, for example, in China, Japan and the Islamic Lands. The Byzantine glassworkers made mould-blown glass decorated with Jewish and Christian symbols in Jerusalem between late sixth century and the middle of the seventh century A.D. Mould-blown vessels with facets, relief and linear-cut decoration were discovered at Samarra in the Islamic Lands.

Recent Developments

The 'studio glass movement' began in 1962 when Harvey Littleton, a ceramics professor, and Dominick Labino, a chemist and engineer, held two workshops at the Toledo Museum of Art, during which they started experimenting with melting glass in a small furnace and creating blown glass art. Thus Littleton and Labino are credited with being the first to make molten glass available to artists working in private studios. This approach to glassblowing blossomed into a worldwide movement, producing such flamboyant and prolific artists as Dale Chihuly, Dante Marioni, Fritz Driesbach and Marvin Lipofsky as well as scores of other modern glass artists. Today there are many different institutions around the world that offer glassmaking resources.

15

Glass Beadmaking

The technology for *glass beadmaking* is among the oldest human arts, dating back 30,000 years. Glass beads have been dated back to at least Roman times. Perhaps the earliest glass-like beads were Egyptian faience beads, a form of clay bead with a self-forming vitreous coating.

Glass beads are usually categorized by the method used to manipulate the glass — wound beads, drawn beads, and molded beads. There are composites, such as millefiori beads, where cross-sections of a drawn glass cane are applied to a wound glass core. A very minor industry in blown glass beads also existed in 19th century Venice and France.

Wound Glass Beads

Probably the earliest beads of true glass were made by the winding method. Glass at a temperature high enough to make it workable, or 'ductile', is laid down or wound around a steel wire or mandrel coated in a clay slip called 'bead release'. The wound bead, while still hot, may be further shaped by manipulating with graphite, wood, stainless steel or marble tools and paddles. This process is called marvering, originating from the French word 'marver' which translates to 'marble'. It can also be pressed into a mold in its molten state. While still hot, or after re-heating, the surface of the bead may be decorated with fine rods called stringers of coloured glass. These are a type of lampwork beads.

Drawn Glass Beads

The drawing of glass is also very ancient. Evidence of large-scale drawn-glass beadmaking has been found by archeologists in India, at sites like Arekamedu dating to the 2nd century CE. The small drawn beads made by that industry have been called Indo-Pacific beads, because they may have been the single most widely traded item in history — found from the islands of the Pacific to Great Zimbabwe in southern Africa.

There are several methods for making drawn beads, but they all involve pulling a strand out of a gather of glass in such a way as to incorporate a bubble in the centre of the strand to serve as the hole in the bead. In Arekamedu this was accomplished by inserting a hollow metal tube into the ball of hot glass and pulling the glass strand out around it, to form a continuous glass tube. In the Venetian bead industry, molten glass was gathered on the end of a tool called a puntile ('puntying up'), a bubble was incorporated into the centre of a gather of molten glass, and a second puntile was attached before stretching the gather with its internal bubble into a long cane. The pulling was a skilled process, and canes were reportedly drawn to lengths up to 200 feet (61 m) long. The drawn tube was then chopped, producing individual drawn beads from its slices. The resulting beads were cooked or rolled in hot sand to round the edges without melting the holes closed; were sieved into sizes; and, usually, strung onto hanks for sale.

The most common type of modern glass bead is the seed bead, a small type of bead typically less than 6 mm, traditionally monochrome, and manufactured in very large quantities.They are a modern example of mechanically-drawn glass beads. The micro-bead or 'seed bead', are so called due to their tiny, regular size. Modern seed beads are extruded by machine and some, such as Miyuki delicas, look like small tubes.

Molded Beads

Pressed or molded beads are associated with higher labour costs. These are made in the Czech republic, in what was once called Bohemia. Thick rods are heated to molten and fed into a complex apparatus that stamps the glass, including a needle that pierces a hole. The beads again are rolled in hot sand to remove flashing and soften seam lines. By making canes (the glass rods fed into the machine) striped or otherwise patterned, the resulting beads can be more elaborately coloured than seed beads. One 'feed' of a hot rod might result in 10-20 beads, and a single operator can make thousands in a day.

The Bohemian glass industry was known for its ability to copy more expensive beads, and produced molded glass 'lion's teeth', 'coral', and 'shells', which were popular in the 19th and early 20th century Africa trade.

A variant of the wound glass beadmaking technique, and a labour intensive one, is what is traditionally called lampworking. In the Venetian industry, where very large quantities of beads were produced in the 19th century for the African trade, the core of a decorated bead was produced from molten glass at furnace temperatures, a large-scale industrial process dominated by men. The delicate multicoloured decoration was then added by people, mostly women, working at home using an oil lamp or spirit lamp to re-heat the cores and the fine wisps of coloured glass used to decorate them. These workers were paid on a piecework basis for the resulting lampwork beads. Modern lampwork beads are made by using a gas torch to heat a rod of glass and spinning the resulting thread around a metal rod covered in bead release. When the base bead has been formed, other colours of glass can be added to the surface to create many designs. After this initial stage of the beadmaking process, the bead can be further fired in a kiln to make it more durable.

Modern beadmakers use single or dual fuel torches, so 'flameworked' is replacing the older term. Unlike a metalworking torch, or burner as some people in the trade prefer to call them, a flameworking torch is usually "surface mix"; that is, the oxygen and fuel (typically propane, though natural gas is also common) is mixed after it comes out of the torch, resulting in a quieter tool and less dirty flame. Also unlike metalworking, the torch is fixed, and the bead and glass move in the flame. American torches are usually mounted at about a 45 degree angle, a result of scientific glassblowing heritage; Japanese torches are recessed, and have flames coming straight up, like a large bunsen burner; Czech production torches tend to be positioned nearly horizontally.

Dichroic Glass Beads

Increasingly, dichroic glass is being used to produce high-end art beads. Dichroic glass has a thin film of metal fused to the surface of the glass, resulting in a surface that has a metallic sheen that changes between two colours when viewed at different angles. Beads can be pressed, or made with traditional lampworking techniques. If the glass is kept in the flame too long, the metallic coating will turn silver and burn off.

Furnace Glass

Italian glass blowing techniques such as latticinio and zanfirico are adapted here to make beads. Furnace glass uses large decorated canes built up out of smaller canes, encased in clear glass and then extruded to form the beads with linear and twisting stripe patterns. No air is blown into the glass. These beads require a large scale glass furnace and annealing kiln for manufacture.

Lead Crystal

Lead crystal beads are machine cut and polished. Their high lead content makes them sparkle more than other glass, but also makes them inherently fragile.

Other Methods for Making Glass Beads

Lead glass (for neon signs) and, especially borosilicate is available in tubing, making true blown beads possible. (Soda-lime glass can be blown at the end of a metal tube, or, more commonly wound on the mandrel to make a hollow bead, but the former is unusual and the latter not a true mouth-blown technique.) In addition, beads can be fused from sheet glass or using ground glass.

Modern Ghana has an industry in beads molded from powdered glass. Also in Africa, Kiffa beads are made in Mauritania, historically by women, using powdered glass that the beadmaker usually grinds herself from commercially available glass seed beads and recycled glass.

Molded ground glass, if painted into the mold, is called pate de verre, and the technique can be used to make beads, though pendants and cabochons are more typical. Lampwork (and other) beads can be painted with glass paints.

16

Roman Glass

Roman glass objects have been recovered across the Roman Empire in domestic, industrial and funerary contexts. Glass was used primarily for the production of vessels, although mosaic tiles and window glass were also produced. Roman glass production developed from Hellenistic technical traditions, initially concentrating on the production of intensely coloured cast glass vessels. However, during the first century AD the industry underwent rapid technical growth that saw the introduction of glass blowing and the dominance of colourless or 'aqua' glasses. Production of raw glass was undertaken in geographically separate locations to the working of glass into finished vessels, and by the end of the first century AD large scale manufacturing resulted in the establishment of glass as a commonly available material in the Roman world.

Despite the growth of glass working in the Hellenistic World and the growing place of glass in material culture, at the beginning of the first century AD there was still no Latin word for it in the Roman World. However, glass was being produced in Roman contexts using primarily Hellenistic techniques and styles by the late Republican period. The majority of manufacturing techniques were time-consuming, and the initial product was a thick-walled vessel which required considerable finishing. This, combined with the cost of importing natron for the production of raw glass, contributed to the limited use of glass and its position as an expensive and high-status material.

The glass industry was therefore a relatively minor craft during the Republican period; although, during the early decades of the first century AD the quantity and diversity of glass vessels available increased dramatically. This was a direct result of the massive growth of the Roman influence at the end of the Republican period, the Pax Romana that followed the decades of civil war, and the stabilisation of the state that occurred under Augustus' rule. Still, Roman glasswares were already making their way through Parthia, Bactria, Fergana, Kashgar, and then to the Han Dynasty of China, as the first Roman glass found in China came from an early 1st century BC tomb at Guangzhou.

In addition to this a major new technique in glass production had been introduced during the first century AD. Glassblowing allowed glass workers to produce vessels with considerably thinner walls, decreasing the amount of glass needed for each vessel. Glass blowing was also considerably quicker than other techniques, and vessels required considerably less finishing, representing a further saving in time, raw material and equipment. Although earlier techniques dominated during the early Augustan and Julio-Claudian periods, by the middle to late first century CE earlier techniques had been largely abandoned in favour of blowing.

As a result of these factors, the cost of production was reduced and glass became available for a wider section of society in a growing variety of forms. By the mid first century AD this meant that glass vessels had moved from a valuable, high-status commodity, to a material commonly available: "a [glass] drinking cup could be bought for a copper coin". This growth also saw the production of the first glass tesserae for mosaics, and the first window glass, as furnace technology improved allowing molten glass to be produced for the first time.

At the same time, the expansion of the empire also brought an influx of people and an expansion of cultural influences that resulted in the adoption of eastern decorative styles. The changes that took place in the Roman glass industry during this period can therefore be seen as a result of three primary influences: historical events, technical innovation and contemporary fashions. They are also linked to the fashions and technologies developed in the ceramic trade, from which a number of forms and techniques were drawn.

Glass making reached its peak at the beginning of the second century AD, with glass objects in domestic contexts of every kind. The primary production techniques of blowing, and to a lesser extent casting, remained in use for the rest of the Roman period, with changes in vessel types but little change in technology. From the second century onwards styles became increasingly regionalised, and evidence indicates that bottles and closed vessels such as unguentaria moved as a by-product of the trade in their contents, and many appear to have matched the Roman scale of liquid measurement. The use of coloured glass as a decorative addition to pale and colourless glasses also increased, and metal vessels continued to influence the shape of glass vessels. After the conversion of Constantine, glass works began to move more quickly from depicting Pagan religious imagery towards adopting scenes from Christian mythology. The movement of the capital to Constantinople rejuvenated the Eastern glass industry, and the presence of the Roman military in the western provinces did much to prevent any downturn there. By the mid fourth century mould-blowing was in use only sporadically.

Roman glass production relied on the application of heat to fuse two primary ingredients: silica and soda.

Technical studies of archaeological glasses divide the ingredients of glass as formers, fluxes, stabilisers, as well as possible opacifiers or colourants.

Former: The major component of the glass is silica, which during the Roman period was sand (quartz), which contains some alumina (typically 2.5%) and nearly 8 per cent lime. Alumina contents vary, peaking around 3 per cent in glasses from the western Empire, and remaining notably lower in glasses from the Middle East.

Flux: This ingredient was used to lower the melting point of the silica to form glass. Analysis of Roman glass has shown that soda was used exclusively in glass production. During this period, the primary source of soda was natron, a naturally occurring salt found in dry lake beds. The main source of natron during the Roman period was Wadi El Natrun, Egypt, although there may have been a source in Italy.

Stabiliser: Glasses formed of silica and soda are naturally soluble, and require the addition of a stabiliser such as lime or magnesia. Lime was the primary stabiliser in use during the Roman period, entering the glass through calcareous particles in the beach sand, rather than as a separate component.

Roman glass has also been shown to contain around 1 per cent to 2 per cent chlorine, in contrast to later glasses. This is thought to have originated either in the addition of salt (NaCl) to reduce the melting temperature and viscosity of the glass, or as a contaminant in the natron.

Archaeological evidence for glass making during the Roman period is scarce, but by drawing comparisons with the later Islamic and Byzantine periods, it is clear that glass making was a significant industry. By the end of the Roman period glass was being produced in large quantities contained in tanks situated inside highly specialised furnaces, as the 8 tonne glass slab recovered from Bet

She-arim illustrates. These workshops could produce many tonnes of raw glass in a single furnace firing, and although this firing might have taken weeks, a single primary workshop could potentially supply multiple secondary glass working sites. It is therefore thought that raw glass production was centred around a relatively small number of workshops, where glass was produced on a large scale and then broken into chunks. There is only limited evidence for local glass making, and only in context of window glass. The development of this large scale industry is not fully understood, but Pliny's Natural History (36, 194), in addition to evidence for the first use of molten glass in the mid first century AD, indicates that furnace technologies experienced marked development during the early to mid first century AD, in tandem with the expansion of glass production.

The siting of glass making workshops was governed by three primary factors; the availability of fuel which was needed in large quantites, sources of sand which represented the major constituent of the glass, and natron to act as a flux. Roman glass relied on natron from Wadi El Natrun, and as a result it is thought that glass making workshops during the Roman period may have been confined to near-coastal regions of the eastern Mediterranean. This facilitated the trade in the raw colourless or naturally coloured glass which they produced, which reached glass working sites across the Roman empire.

The scarcity of archaeological evidence for Roman glass making facilities has resulted in the use of chemical compositions as evidence for production models, as the division of production indicates that any variation is related to differences in raw glass making. However, the Roman reliance on natron from Wadi El Natrun as a flux, has resulted in a largely homogenous composition in the majority of Roman glasses. Despite the publication of major analyses, comparisons of chemical analyses produced by different analytical methods have only recently been attempted, and although there is some variation in Roman glass compositions, meaningful compositional groups have been difficult to establish for this period.

The Roman writers Statius and Martial both indicate that recycling broken glass was an important part of the glass industry, and this seems to be supported by the fact that only rarely are glass fragments of any size recovered from domestic sites of this period. In the western empire there is evidence that recycling of broken glass was frequent and extensive(cullet), and that quantities of broken glassware were concentrated at local sites prior to melting back into raw glass. Compositionally, repeated recycling is visible via elevated levels of those metals used as colourants.

Melting does not appear to have taken place in crucibles; rather, cooking pots appear to have been used for small scale operations. For larger work, large tanks or tank-like ceramic containers were utilised. In the largest cases, large furnaces were built to surround these tanks.

Glass Working

In comparison to glass making, there is evidence for glass working in many locations across the empire. Unlike the making process, the working of glass required significantly lower temperatures and substantially less fuel. As a result of this and the expansion of the Empire, glass working sites developed in Rome, Campania and the Po Valley by the end of the first century BC, producing the new blown vessels alongside cast vessels. Italy is known to have been a centre for the working and export of brightly coloured vessels at this time, with production peaking during the mid first century AD.

By the early to mid first century AD, the growth of the Empire saw the establishment of glass working sites at locations along trade routes, with Cologne and other Rhineland centres becoming important glass working sites from the Imperial period, and Syrian glass being exported as far as Italy. During this period vessel forms varied between workshops, with areas such as the Rhineland and northern France producing distinctive forms which are not seen further south. Growth in the industry continued into the third century CE, when sites at the Colonia Claudia Agrippinensis appear to have experienced significant expansion, and by the third and early fourth centuries producers north of the Alps were exporting down to the north of Italy and the transalpine regions.

Glass working sites such as those at Aquileia also had an important role in the spread of glassworking traditions and the trade in materials that used hollow glasswares as containers. However, by the fourth and fifth centuries Italian glass workshops predominate.

The earliest Roman glass follows Hellenistic traditions and uses strongly coloured and 'mosaic' patterned glass. During the late Republican period new highly coloured striped wares with a fusion of dozens of monochrome and lace-work strips were introduced. During this period there is some evidence that styles of glass varied geographically, with the translucent coloured fine wares of the early first century notably 'western' in origin, whilst the later colourless fine wares are more 'international'. These objects also represent the first with a distinctly Roman style unrelated to the Hellenistic casting traditions on which they are based, and are characterised by novel rich colours. 'Emerald' green, dark or cobalt blue, a deep blue-green and Persian or 'peacock' blue are most commonly associated with this period, and other colours are very rare. Of these, Emerald green and peacock blue were new colours introduced by the Romano-Italian industry and almost exclusively associated with the production of fine wares.

However, during the last thirty years of the first century AD there was a marked change in style, with strong colours disappearing rapidly, replaced by 'aqua' and true colourless glasses. Colourless and 'aqua' glasses had been in use for vessels and some mosaic designs prior to his, but start to dominate the blown glass market at this time. The use of strong colours in cast glass died out during this period, with colourless or 'aqua' glasses dominating the last class of cast vessels to be produced in quantity, as mould and free-blowing took over during the first century AD.

From around 70 AD colourless glass becomes the predominate material for fine wares, and the cheaper glasses move towards pale shades of blue, green, and yellow. Debate continues whether this change in fashion indicates a change in attitude that placed glass as individual material of merit no longer required to imitate precious stones, ceramics of metal, or whether the shift to colourless glass indicated an attempt to mimic highly prized rock crystal. Pliny, in his Historia Naturalis, states that "the most highly valued glass is colourless and transparent, as closely as possible resembling rock crystal" (36, 192), which is thought to support this last position, as is evidence for the persistence of casting as a production technique, which produced the thickly walled vessels necessary to take the pressure of extensive cutting and polishing associated with crystal working.

Artisans used a mass of mud and straw fixed around a metal rod to form a core, and built up a vessel by either dipping the core in liquified glass, or by trailing liquid glass over the core. The core was removed after the glass had cooled, and handles, rims and bases were then added. These vessels are characterised by relatively thick walls, bright colours and zigzagging patterns of contrasting colours, and were limited in size to small unguent or scent containers. This early technique continued in popularity during the first century BCE, despite the earlier introduction of slumped and cast vessels.

Cold-cut Vessels

This technique is related to the origin of glass as a substitute for gemstones. By borrowing techniques for stone and carved gems, artisans were able to produce a variety of small containers from blocks of raw glass or thick moulded blanks, including cameo glass in two or more colours.

These techniques, which were to dominate the Roman glass working industry after the late first century AD, are discussed in detail on the glass blowing page. Mould-blown glass appears in the second quarter of the first century AD.

The glass sheets used for slumping could be produced of plain or multicoloured glass, or even formed of 'mosaic' pieces. The production of these objects later developed into the modern caneworking and millefiori techniques, but is noticeably different. Four primary patterns of 'mosaic' glass have been identified:

- ***Floral (millefiori) and spiral patterns:*** This was produced by binding rods of coloured glass together and heating and fusing them into a single piece. These were then cut in cross-section, and the resulting discs could be fused together to create complex patterns. Alternately, two strips of contrasting-coloured glass could be fused together, and then wound round a glass rod whilst still hot to produce a spiral pattern. Cross-sections of this were also cut, and could be fused together to form a plate or fused to plain glass.
- ***Marbled and dappled patterns:*** Some of these patterns are clearly formed through the distortion of the original pattern during the slumping of the glass plate during melting However, by using spiral and circular patterns of alternating colours producers were also able to deliberately imitate the appearance of natural stones such as sardonyx. This occurs most often on pillar-moulded bowls, which are one of the commonest glass finds on first century sites.
- ***Lace patterns:*** Strips of coloured glass were twisted with a contrasting coloured thread of glass before being fused together. This was a popular method in the early period, but appears to have gone out of fashion by the mid first century AD.

- ***Striped patterns:*** Lengths of monochrome and lacework glass were fused together to create vivid striped designs, a technique that developed from the lace pattern technique during the last decades of the first century AD.

The production of multicoloured vessels declined after the mid first century, but remained in use for some time after.

Shards of broken glass or glass rods were being used in mosaics from the Augustan period onwards, but by the beginning of the first century small glass tiles (tesserae) were being produced specifically for use in mosaics. These were usually in shades of yellow, blue or green, and were predominantly used in mosaics laid under fountains or as highlights.

Around the same time the first window panes are thought to have been produced. The earliest panes were rough cast into a wooden frame on top of a layer of sand or stone, but from the late third century onwards window glass was made by the muff process, where a blown cylinder was cut laterally and flattened out to produce a sheet.

Aqua', a pale blue-green colour, is the common natural colour of untreated glass. Many early Roman vessels are this colour (Fe_2O_3) Colourless glass was produced in the Roman period by adding manganese oxide. This oxidised the iron (II) oxide to iron (III) oxide, which although yellow, is a much weaker colourant, allowing the glass to appear colourless. The use of manganese as a decolourant was a Roman invention first noted in the Imperial period; prior to this, antimony-rich minerals were used. Amber Iron-sulfur compounds 0.2 per cent-1.4 per cent S 0.3 per cent Fe Sulfur is likely to have entered the glass as a contaminant of natron, producing a green tinge. Formation of iron-sulfur compounds produces an amber colour.

The natural 'aqua' shade can be intensified with the addition of copper. During the Roman period this was derived from the recovery of oxide scale from scrap copper when heated, to avoid the contaminants present in copper minerals. Copper produced a translucent blue moving towards a darker and denser green. Oxidising Dark green Lead By adding lead, the green colour produced by copper could be darkened. Royal blue to navy Cobalt 0.1 per cent Intense colouration Powder blue Egyptian blue Opaque red to brown (Pliny's Haematinum) Copper lead >10 per cent Cu 1 per cent - 20 per cent Pb Under strongly reducing conditions, copper present in the glass will precipitate inside the matrix as cuprous oxide, making the glass appear brown to blood red. Lead encourages precipitation and brilliance. The red is a rare find, but is known to have been in production during the fourth, fifth and later centuries on the continent. Strongly reducing White Antimony (such as stibnite) 1-10 per cent Antimony reacts with the lime in the glass matrix to precipitate calcium antimonite crystals creating a white with high opacity. Oxidising Yellow Antimony and lead (such as bindheimite). Precipitation of lead pyroantimonate creates an opaque yellow. Yellow rarely appears alone in Roman glass, but was used for the mosaic and polychrome pieces.

These colours formed the basis of all Roman glass, and although some of them required high technical ability and knowledge, a degree of uniformity was achieved.

17

Glass-reinforced Plastic

Glass-reinforced Plastic or *GRP* is a composite material made of a plastic matrix reinforced by fine fibres made of glass. It is also known as *GFK* (for Glass Fibre Komposit), or simply by the name of the reinforcing fibres themselves: *fibreglass.*

GRP is a lightweight, strong material with very many uses, including boats, automobiles, water tanks, roofing, pipes and cladding.

The plastic matrix may be a thermosetting plastic (most often polyester or vinylester), epoxy or thermoplastic.

The manufacturing process for GRP fibre glass uses large furnaces to gradually melt the sand/chemical mix to liquid form, then extrude it through bundles of very small orifices (typically 17-25 micrometres in diametre for E-Glass, 9 micrometres for S-Glass). These filaments are then *sized* with a chemical solution. The individual filaments are now bundled together in large numbers to provide a *roving.* The diameter of the filaments, as well as the number of filaments in the roving determine its *weight.* This is typically expressed in yield-yards per pound (how many yards of fibre in one pound of material, thus a smaller number means a heavier roving, example of standard yields are 225 yield, 450yield, 675yield) or in tex-grams per km (how many grams 1 km of roving weighs, this is inverted from yield, thus a smaller number means a lighter roving, examples of standard tex are 750tex, 1100tex, 2200tex).

These rovings are then either used directly in a composite application such as pultrusion, filament wounding (pipe), gun roving (automated gun chops the glass into small lengths and drops it into a jet of resin, projected onto the surface of a mold), or used in an intermediary step, to manufacture fabrics such as chopped strand mat (CSM) (made of randomly oriented small cut lengths of fibre all bonded together), woven fabrics, knit fabrics or uni-directional fabrics.

Sizing

A sort of coating, or primer, which both helps protect the glass filaments for processing/manipulation as well as ensure proper bonding to the resin matrix, thus allowing for transfer of shear loads from the glass fibres (which would buckle) to the thermoset plastic (which is quite good at handling shear loads), without this 'bonding', the fibres can 'slip' in the matrix and localised failure will ensue. (Citation needed | date=August 2009). Usually also the basic material for making cloth.

An individual structural glass fibre is both stiff and strong in tension and compression – that is, along its axis. Although it might be assumed that the fibre is weak in compression, it is actually only the long aspect ratio of the fibre which makes it seem so; i.e., because a typical fibre is long and narrow, it buckles easily. On the other hand, the glass fibre is unstiff and unstrong in shear — that is, across its axis. Therefore if a collection of fibres can be arranged permanently in a preferred direction within a material, and if the fibres can be prevented from buckling in compression, then that material will become preferentially strong in that direction.

Furthermore, by laying multiple layers of fibre on top of one another, with each layer oriented in various preferred directions, the stiffness and strength properties of the overall material can be controlled in an efficient manner. In the case of glass-reinforced plastic, it is the plastic matrix which permanently constrains the structural glass fibres to directions chosen by the designer. With chopped strand mat, this directionality is essentially an entire two dimensional plane; with woven fabrics or unidirectional layers, directionality of stiffness and strength can be more precisely controlled within the plane.

A glass-reinforced plastic component is typically of a thin "shell" construction, sometimes filled on the inside with structural foam, as in the case of surfboards. The component may be of nearly arbitrary shape, limited only by the complexity and tolerances of the mold used for manufacturing the shell.

Applications

GRP is an immensely versatile material which combines lightweight with inherent strength to provide a weather resistant finish, with a variety of surface texture and an unlimited colour range available.

GRP was developed in the UK during the Second World War as a replacement for the molded plywood used in aircraft radomes (GRP being transparent to microwaves). Its first main civilian application was for building of boats, where it gained acceptance in the 1950s. Its use has broadened to the automotive and sport equipment sectors as well as model aircraft, although its use there is now partly being taken over by carbon fibre which weighs less per given volume and is stronger both by volume and by weight. GRP uses also include hot tubs, pipes for drinking water and sewers, office plant display containers and flat roof systems.

Advanced manufacturing techniques such as pre-pregs and fibre rovings extend the applications and the tensile strength possible with fibre-reinforced plastics.

GRP is also used in the telecommunications industry for shrouding the visual appearance of antennas, due to its RF permeability and low signal attenuation properties. It may also be used to shroud the visual appearance of other equipment where no signal permeability is required, such as equipment cabinets and steel support structures, due to the ease with which it can be molded, manufactured and painted to custom designs, to blend in with existing structures or brickwork. Other uses include sheet form made electrical insulators and other structural components commonly found in the power industries.

Storage Tanks

Storage tanks can be made of GRP with capacities up to about 300 tonnes. The smaller tanks can be made with chopped strand mat cast over a thermoplastic inner tank which acts as a preform during construction. Much more reliable tanks are made using woven mat or filament wound fibre with the fibre orientation at right angles to the hoop stress imposed in the side wall by the contents. They tend to be used for chemical storage because the plastic liner (often polypropylene) is resistant to a wide range of strong chemicals. GRP tanks are also used for septic tanks.

House Building

Glass reinforced plastics are also used in the house building market for the production of roofing laminate, door surrounds, over-door canopies, window canopies and dormers, chimneys, coping systems, heads with keystones and sills. The use of GRP for these applications provides for a much faster installation and due to the reduced weight manual handling issues are reduced. With the advent of high volume manufacturing processes it is possible to construct GRP brick effect panels which can be used in the construction of composite housing. These panels can be constructed with the appropriate insulation which reduces heat loss.

Resin is mixed with a catalyst (e.g. butanox LA) or hardener if working with epoxy, otherwise it will not cure (harden) for days/ weeks. Next, the mold is wetted out with the mixture. The sheets of fibreglass are placed over the mold and rolled down into the mold using steel rollers. The material must be securely attached to the mold, air must not be trapped in between the fibreglass and the mold. Additional resin is applied and possibly additional sheets of fibreglass. Rollers are used to make sure the resin is between all the layers, the glass is wetted throughout the entire thickness of the laminate, and any air pockets are removed. The work must be done quickly enough to complete the job before the resin starts to cure. Various curing times can be achieved by altering the amount of catalyst employed.

Fibreglass Spray Lay-up Operation

The fibreglass spray lay-up process is similar to the hand lay-up process but the difference comes from the application of the fibre and resin material to the mold. Spray-up is an open-molding composites fabrication process where resin and reinforcements are sprayed onto a mold. The resin and glass may be applied separately or simultaneously 'chopped' in a combined stream from a chopper gun. Workers roll out the spray-up to compact the laminate. Wood, foam or other core material may then be added, and a secondary spray-up layer imbeds the core between the laminates. The part is then cured, cooled and removed from the reusable mold.

Pultrusion is a manufacturing method used to make strong light weight composite materials, in this case fibreglass. Fibres (the glass material) are pulled from spools through a device that coats them with a resin. They are then typically heat treated and cut to length. Pultrusions can be made in a variety of shapes or cross-sections such as a W or S cross-section. The word pultrusion describes the method of moving the fibres through the machinery. It is pulled through using either a hand over hand method or a continuous roller method. This is opposed to an extrusion which would push the material through dies.

Chopped Strand Mat

Chopped strand mat or *CSM* is a form of reinforcement used in glass-reinforced plastic. It consists of glass-fibres laid randomly across each other and held together by a binder.

It is typically processed using the hand lay-up technique, where sheets of material are placed in a mold and brushed with resin. Because the binder dissolves in resin, the material easily conforms to different shapes when wetted out. After the resin cures, the hardened product can be taken from the mold and finished.

Using chopped strand mat gives a glass-reinforced plastic with isotropic in-plane material properties.

18

Amorphous Solid

An 'amorphous solid' is a solid in which there is no long-range order of the positions of the atoms. (Solids in which there is long-range atomic order are called crystallines or morphous). Most classes of solid materials can be found or prepared in an amorphous form. For instance, common window glass is an amorphous solid, many polymers (such as polystyrene) are amorphous, and even foods such as cotton candy are amorphous solids.

In principle, given a sufficiently high cooling rate, any liquid can be made into an amorphous solid. Cooling reduces molecular mobility. If the cooling rate is faster than the rate at which molecules can organize into a more thermodynamically favourable crystalline state, then an amorphous solid will be formed. Because of entropy considerations, many polymers can be made amorphous solids by cooling even at slow rates. In contrast, if molecules have sufficient time to organize into a structure with two- or three-dimensional order, then a crystalline (or semi-crystalline) solid will be formed. Water is one example. Because of its small molecular size and ability to quickly rearrange, it cannot be made amorphous without resorting to specialized hyperquenching techniques.

Amorphous materials can also be produced by additives which interfere with the ability of the primary constituent to crystallize. For example, addition of soda to silicon dioxide results in window glass, and the addition of glycols to water results in a vitrified solid.

Some materials, such as metals, are difficult to prepare in an amorphous state. Unless a material has a high melting temperature (as ceramics do) or a low crystallization energy (as polymers tend to), cooling must be done extremely rapidly. As the cooling is performed, the material changes from a supercooled liquid, with properties one would expect from a liquid state material, to a solid. The temperature at which this transition occurs is called the glass transition temperature or T_g.

It is difficult to make a distinction between truly amorphous solids and crystalline solids if the size of the crystals is very small. Even amorphous materials have some short-range order at the atomic length scale due the nature of chemical bonding. Furthermore, in very small crystals a large fraction of the atoms are located at or near the surface of the crystal; relaxation of the surface and interfacial effects distort the atomic positions, decreasing the structural order. Even the most advanced structural characterization techniques, such as x-ray diffraction and transmission electron microscopy, have difficulty in distinguishing between amorphous and crystalline structures on these length scales.

The transition from the liquid state to the glass, at a temperature below the equilibrium melting point of the material, is called the glass transition. The glass transition temperature, Tg, is the temperature at which an amorphous solid, such as glass or a polymer, becomes brittle on cooling, or soft on heating. More specifically, it defines a pseudo second order phase transition in which a supercooled melt yields, on cooling, a glassy structure and properties similar to those of crystalline materials e.g. of an isotropic solid material. T_g is usually applicable to wholly or partially amorphous solids such as common glasses and plastics (organic polymers). Below the glass transition temperature,

Tg, amorphous solids are in a glassy state and most of their joining bonds are intact. In inorganic glasses, with increased temperature more and more joining bonds are broken by thermal fluctuations so that broken bonds (termed configurons) begin to form clusters. Above T_g these clusters become macroscopic large facilitating the flow of material. In organic polymers, secondary, non-covalent bonds between the polymer chains become weak above T_g. Above T_g glasses and organic polymers become soft and capable of plastic deformation without fracture. This behaviour is one of the things which make most plastics useful . It is important to note that the glass transition temperature is a kinetic parameter, and thus parametrically depends on the melt cooling rate. Thus the slower the melt cooling rate, the lower T_g. In addition, T_g depends on the measurement conditions, which are not universally defined. The glass transition temperature is approximately the temperature at which the viscosity of the liquid exceeds a certain value (about 10^{12} Pa·s). The transition temperature depends on cooling rate, with the glass transition occurring at higher temperatures for faster cooling rates. The precise nature of the glass transition is the subject of ongoing research. While it is clear that the glass transition is not a first-order thermodynamic transition (such as melting), there is debate as to whether it is a higher-order transition such percolation type transformation, or merely a kinetic effect.

Amorphous phases are important constituents of thin films, which are solid layers of a few nm to some tens of µm thickness deposited upon an underlying substrate. So-called structure zone models were developed to describe the microstructure and morphology of thin films as a function of the homologeous temperature T_h that is the ratio of deposition temperature over melting temperature . According to these models, a necessary (but not sufficient) condition for the occurrence of amorphous phases is that T_h has to be smaller than 0.3, that is the deposition temperature must be below 30 per cent of the melting temperature. For higher values, the surface diffusion of deposited atomic species would allow for the formation of crystallites with long range atomic order.

Regarding their applications, amorphous metallic layers played an important role in the discussion of a suspected superconductivity in amorphous metals . Today, optical coatings made from TiO_2, SiO_2, Ta_2O_5 etc. and combinations of them in most cases comprise of amorphous phases of these compounds. Much research is carried out into thin amorphous films as a gas separating membrane layer . The technologically most important thin amorphous film is probably represented by few nm thin SiO_2 layers serving as isolator above the conducting channel of a metal-oxide semiconductor field-effect transistor MOSFET. Also, hydrogenated amorphous silicon, a-Si:H in short, is of technical significance for thin film solar cells. In case of a-Si:H the missing long-range order between silicon atoms is partly induced by the presence by hydrogen in the per cent range.

The occurrence of amorphous phases turned out as a phenomenon of particular interest for studying thin film growth. Remarkably, the growth of polycrystalline films is often preceded by an initial amorphous layer, the thickness of which may amount to only a few nm. The most investigated example is represented by thin multicrystalline silicon films, where such an initial amorphous layer was observed in many studies, see for instance. Wedge-shaped polycrystals were identified by transmission electron microscopy to grow out of the amorphous phase only after the latter has exceeded a certain thickness, the precise value of which depends on deposition temperature, background pressure and various other process parameters. The phenomenon has been interpreted in the framework of Ostwald's rule of stages that predicts the formation of phases to proceed with increasing condensation time towards increasing stability. Experimental studies of the phenomenon require a clearly defined state of the substrate surface and its contaminant density etc., upon which the thin film is deposited.

19

Lens (Optics)

A *lens* is an optical device with perfect or approximate axial symmetry which transmits and refracts light, converging or diverging the beam. A simple lens consists of a single optical element. A *compound lens* is an array of simple lenses (elements) with a common axis; the use of multiple elements allows more optical aberrations to be corrected than is possible with a single element. Lenses are typically made of glass or transparent plastic. Elements which refract electromagnetic radiation outside the visual spectrum are also called lenses: for instance, a microwave lens can be made from paraffin wax.

The variant spelling *lense* is sometimes seen. While it is listed as an alternative spelling in some dictionaries, most mainstream dictionaries do not list it as acceptable.

The oldest lens artifact is the Nimrud lens, which is over three thousand years old, dating back to ancient Assyria. David Brewster proposed that it may have been used as a magnifying glass, or as a burning-glass to start fires by concentrating sunlight. Assyrian craftsmen made intricate engravings, and could have used such a lens in their work. Another early reference to magnification dates back to ancient Egyptian hieroglyphs in the 8th century BC, which depict 'simple glass meniscal lenses'.

The earliest written records of lenses date to Ancient Greece, with Aristophanes' play *The Clouds* (424 BC) mentioning a burning-glass (a biconvex lens used to focus the sun's rays to produce fire). The writings of Pliny the Elder (23-79) also show that burning-glasses were known to the Roman Empire, and mentions what is arguably the earliest use of a corrective lens: Nero was said to watch the gladiatorial games using an emerald (presumably concave to correct for myopia, though the reference is vague). Both Pliny and Seneca the Younger (3 BC-65) described the magnifying effect of a glass globe filled with water.

The word *lens* comes from the Latin name of the lentil, because a double-convex lens is lentil-shaped. The genus of the lentil plant is *Lens*, and the most commonly eaten species is *Lens culinaris*. The lentil plant also gives its name to a geometric figure.

The Arab physicist and mathematician Ibn Sahl (c.940-c.1000) used what is now known as Snell's law to calculate the shape of lenses. Ibn al-Haytham (965-1038), known in the West as *Alhazen*, wrote the first major optical treatise, the *Book of Optics*, which contained the earliest historical proof of a magnifying device, a convex lens forming a magnified image. The book was translated into Latin in the 12th century, and became the standard textbook in the field and influenced many other writers.

Excavations at the Viking harbour town of Fröjel, Gotland, Sweden discovered in 1999 the rock crystal Visby lenses, produced by turning on pole-lathes at Fröjel in the 11th to 12th century, with an imaging quality comparable to that of 1950s aspheric lenses. The Viking lenses concentrate sunlight enough to ignite fires.

Widespread use of lenses did not occur until the use of reading stones in the 11th century and the invention of spectacles, probably in Italy in the 1280s. Scholars have noted that spectacles were invented not long after the translation of al-Haytham's book into Latin, but it is not clear what role, if any, the optical theory of the time played in the discovery. Nicholas of Cusa is believed to have been the first to discover the benefits of concave lenses for the treatment of myopia in 1451.

The Abbe sine condition, due to Ernst Abbe (1860s), is a condition that must be fulfilled by a lens or other optical system in order for it to produce sharp images of off-axis as well as on-axis objects. It revolutionized the design of optical instruments such as microscopes, and helped to establish the Carl Zeiss company as a leading supplier of optical instruments.

Construction of Simple Lenses

Most lenses are *spherical lenses*: their two surfaces are parts of the surfaces of spheres, with the lens axis ideally perpendicular to both surfaces. Each surface can be *convex* (bulging outwards from the lens), *concave* (depressed into the lens), or *planar* (flat). The line joining the centres of the spheres making up the lens surfaces is called the *axis* of the lens. Typically the lens axis passes through the physical centre of the lens, because of the way they are manufactured. Lenses may be cut or ground after manufacturing to give them a different shape or size. The lens axis may then not pass through the physical centre of the lens.

Toric or sphero-cylindrical lenses have surfaces with two different radii of curvature in two orthogonal planes. They have a different focal power in different meridians. This is a form of deliberate astigmatism.

More complex are aspheric lenses. These are lenses where one or both surfaces have a shape that is neither spherical nor cylindrical. Such lenses can produce images with much less aberration than standard simple lenses.

Lenses are classified by the curvature of the two optical surfaces. A lens is *biconvex* (or *double convex*, or just *convex*) if both surfaces are convex. If both surfaces have the same radius of curvature, the lens is *equiconvex*. A lens with two concave surfaces is *biconcave* (or just *concave*). If one of the surfaces is flat, the lens is *plano-convex* or *plano-concave* depending on the curvature of the other surface. A lens with one convex and one concave side is *convex-concave* or *meniscus*. It is this type of lens that is most commonly used in corrective lenses.

If the lens is biconvex or plano-convex, a collimated or parallel beam of light travelling parallel to the lens axis and passing through the lens will be converged (or *focussed*) to a spot on the axis, at a certain distance behind the lens (known as the *focal length*). In this case, the lens is called a *positive* or *converging* lens.

Lenses are used as prosthetics for the correction of visual impairments such as myopia, hyperopia, presbyopia, and astigmatism. Most lenses used for other purposes have strict axial symmetry; eyeglass lenses are only approximately symmetric. They are usually shaped to fit in a roughly oval, not circular, frame; the optical centers are placed over the eyeballs; their curvature may not be axially symmetric to correct for astigmatism. Sunglasses' lenses are designed to attenuate light; sunglass lenses that also correct visual impairments can be custom made.

Other uses are in imaging systems such as monoculars, binoculars, telescopes, microscopes, cameras and projectors. Some of these instruments produce a virtual image when applied to the human eye; others produce a real image which can be captured on photographic film or an optical sensor, or can be viewed on a screen. In these devices lenses are sometimes paired up with curved mirrors to make a catadioptric system where the lenses spherical aberration corrects the opposite aberration in the mirror (such as Schmidt and meniscus correctors).

Convex lenses produce an image of an object at infinity at their focus; if the sun is imaged, much of the visible and infrared light incident on the lens is concentrated into the small image. A large lens will create enough intensity to burn a flammable object at the focal point. Since ignition can be achieved even with a poorly made lens, lenses have been used as burning-glasses for at least 2400 years. A modern application is the use of relatively large lenses to concentrate solar energy on relatively small photovoltaic cells, harvesting more energy without the need to use larger, more expensive, cells.

Radio astronomy and radar systems often use dielectric lenses, commonly called a lens antenna to refract electromagnetic radiation into a collector antenna. The Square Kilometre Array radio telescope, scheduled to be operational by 2020, will employ such lenses to get a collection area nearly 30 times greater than any previous antenna.

Lenses can become scratched and abraded. Abrasion resistant coatings are available to help control this.

20

Transparency and Translucency

In the field of optics, *transparency* (also called *pellucidity* or *diaphaneity*) is the physical property of allowing light to pass through a material; *translucency* (also called *translucence* or *translucidity*) only allows light to pass through diffusely. The opposite property is opacity. Transparent materials are clear, while translucent ones cannot be seen through clearly.

When light encounters a material, it can interact with it in several different ways. These interactions depend on the nature of the light (its wavelength, frequency, energy, etc.) and the nature of the material. Light waves interact with an object by some combination of reflection, and transmission with refraction.

Some materials, such as plate glass and clean water, allow much of the light that falls on them to be transmitted, with little being reflected; such materials are called optically transparent. Many liquids and aqueous solutions are highly transparent. Absence of structural defects (voids, cracks, etc.) and molecular structure of most liquids are mostly responsible for excellent optical transmission.

Materials which do not allow the transmission of light are called opaque. Many such substances have a chemical composition which includes what are referred to as absorption centers. Many substances are selective in their absorption of white light frequencies. They absorb certain portions of the visible spectrum, while reflecting others. The frequencies of the spectrum which are not absorbed are either reflected back or transmitted for our physical observation. This is what gives rise to colour. The attenuation of light of all frequencies and wavelengths is due to the combined mechanisms of absorption and scattering.

With regards to the absorption of light, primary material considerations include:

- At the electronic level, absorption in the ultraviolet and visible (UV-Vis) portions of the spectrum depends on whether the electron orbitals are spaced (or "quantizéd") such that they can absorb a quantum of light (or photon) of a specific frequency, and does not violate selection rules. For example, in most glasses, electrons have no available energy levels above them in range of that associated with visible light, or if they do, they violate selection rules. Thus, there is no appreciable absorption in pure (undoped) glasses, making them ideal transparent materials for windows in buildings.
- At the atomic or molecular level, physical absorption in the infrared portion of the spectrum depends on the frequencies of atomic or molecular vibrations or chemical bonds, and on selection rules. Nitrogen and oxygen are not greenhouse gases because the absorption is forbidden by the lack of a molecular dipole moment.

With regards to the scattering of light, the most critical factor is the length scale of any or all of these structural features relative to the wavelength of the light being scattered. Primary material considerations include:

- ***Crystalline structure:*** How close-packed its atoms or molecules are, and whether or not the atoms or molecules exhibit the *long-range order* evidenced in crystalline solids.

- ***Glassy structure:*** Scattering centers include fluctuations in density and/or composition.
- ***Microstructure:*** Scattering centres include internal surfaces such as grains, grain boundaries, and microscopic pores.

Radiant energy is energy which is propagated in the form of Electromagnetic waves. The type of light which we perceive through our optical sensors (eyes) is referred to as white light, and it is composed of a range of colours (ROYGB: red, orange, yellow, green, blue) over a range of wavelengths, or frequencies. Visible (white) light is only a small fraction of the entire spectrum of electromagnetic radiation. At the short end of that wavelength scale is invisible ultraviolet (UV) light. At even shorter wavelengths than UV are X-rays and gamma-rays. At the longer end of that spectrum is infrared (IR) light, which is used for night vision and other heat-seeking devices. At longer wavelengths than infrared are microwaves (radar), and radio/television waves.

Electromagnetic radiation is classified according to the frequency (or wavelength, which is inversely proportional to the frequency) of the light. This includes (in order of increasing frequency): radio waves, microwaves, terahertz radiation, infrared radiation, visible light, ultraviolet (UV) radiation, X-rays and gamma rays. Of these, radio waves have the longest wavelengths and gamma rays have the shortest. A small window of frequencies, called the visible (or white light) portion of the spectrum, is sensed by the naked eye of various organisms.

The simplest representation of a beam of light is through the use of the light ray. The most important properties of the light ray are that it contains no mass and that it travels along a straight line. Light rays interact with the materials (liquids and solids) in several different ways; it is absorbed, reflected or transmitted by the object. In the case of reflection, the interaction depends on the physical and chemical properties of the substance. If the materials surface is perfectly smooth (e.g. a mirror), rays of light collectively undergo total reflection (or specular reflection), leaving the surface of the glass at a particular angle and all in a parallel line with each other.

Light Scattering

Rough and irregular surfaces cause light rays to be reflected in many random directions. This type of reflection is called "diffuse reflection", and is typically characterized by wide variety of reflection angles. Most of the objects visible to the naked eye are identified via diffuse reflection. Another term commonly used for this type of reflection is 'light scattering'. *Light scattering from the surfaces of objects is our primary mechanism of physical observation.*

Light scattering in liquids and solids therefore depends on the wavelength of the light being scattered. Limits to spatial scales of visibility (using white light) therefore arise, depending on the frequency of the light wave and the physical dimension (or spatial scale) of the scattering centre. For example, since visible light has a wavelength scale on the order of a micrometre (one millionth of a metre) scattering centres (or particles) as small as one micrometre have been observed directly in the light microscope (e.g. Brownian motion).

When light strikes an object, it usually has not just a single frequency (or wavelength) but many. Objects have a tendency to selectively absorb, reflect or transmit light of certain frequencies. That is, one object might reflect green light while absorbing all other frequencies of visible light. Another object might selectively transmit blue light while absorbing all other frequencies of visible light. The manner in which visible light interacts with an object is dependent upon the frequency of the light, the nature of the atoms in the object, and often the nature of the electrons in the atoms of the object.

Some materials allow much of the light that falls on them to be transmitted through the material without being reflected. Materials that allow the transmission of light waves through them are called optically transparent. Chemically pure (undoped) window glass and clean river or spring water are prime examples of this.

Materials which do not allow the transmission of any light wave frequencies are called opaque. Such substances have a chemical composition which includes what are referred to as absorption centers. Most materials are composed of materials which are selective in their absorption of white light frequencies. Thus they absorb certain portions of the visible spectrum, while reflecting others. The frequencies of the spectrum which are not absorbed are either reflected back or transmitted for our physical observation. In the visible portion of the spectrum, this is what gives rise to colour.

Colour centres are largely responsible for the appearance of specific wavelengths of visible light all around us. Moving from longer (0.7 micrometre) to shorter (0.4 micrometre) wavelengths: red, orange, yellow, green and blue (ROYGB) can all be identified by our senses in the appearance of colour by the selective absorption of specific light wave frequencies (or wavelengths). Mechanisms of selective light wave absorption include:

- ***Electronic:*** Transitions in electron energy levels within the atom (e.g. pigments). These transitions are typically in the ultraviolet (UV) and/or visible portions of the spectrum.
- **Vibrational:** Resonance in atomic/molecular vibrational modes. These transitions are typically in the infrared portion of the spectrum.

In electronic absorption, the frequency of the incoming light wave is at or near the energy levels of the electrons within the atoms which compose the substance. In this case, the electrons will absorb the energy of the light wave and increase their energy state, often moving outward from the nucleus of the atom into an outer shell or orbital.

The atoms that bind together to make the molecules of any particular substance contain a number of electrons (given by the atomic number Z in the periodic chart). Recall that all light waves are electromagnetic in origin. Thus they are affected strongly when coming into contact with negatively charged electrons in matter. When photons (individual packets of light energy) come in contact with the valence electrons of atom, one of several things can and will occur:

- An electron absorbs all of the energy of the photon and re-emits it with different colour. This gives rise to luminescence, fluorescence and phosphorescence.
- An electron absorbs the energy of the photon and sends it back out the way it came in. This results in reflection or scattering.
- An electron cannot absorb the energy of the photon and the photon continues on its path. This results in transmission (provided no other absorption mechanisms are active).
- An electron selectively absorbs a portion of the photon, and the remaining frequencies are transmitted in the form of spectral colour.

Most of the time, it is a combination of the above that happens to the light that hits an object. The electrons in different materials vary in the range of energy that they can absorb. Most glasses, for example, blocks ultraviolet (UV) light. What happens is the electrons in the glass absorb the energy of the photons in the UV range while ignoring the weaker energy of photons in the visible light spectrum.

Thus, when a material is illuminated, individual photons of light can make the valence electrons of an atom transition to a higher electronic energy level. The photon is destroyed in the process and the absorbed radiant energy is transformed to electric potential energy. Several things can happen then to the absorbed energy. as it may be re-emitted by the electron as radiant energy (in this case the overall effect is in fact a scattering of light), dissipated to the rest of the material (i.e. transformed into heat), or the electron can be freed from the atom (as in the photoelectric and Compton effects).

The primary physical mechanism for storing mechanical energy of motion in condensed matter is through heat, or thermal energy. Thermal energy manifests itself as energy of motion. Thus, heat is motion at the atomic and molecular levels. The primary mode of motion in crystalline substances is vibration. Any given atom will vibrate around some mean or average position within a crystalline structure, surrounded by its nearest neighbours. This vibration in 2-dimensions is equivalent to the oscillation of a clock's pendulum. It swings back and forth symmetrically about some mean or average (vertical) position. Atomic and molecular vibrational frequencies may average on the order of 10^{12} cycles per second (hertz).

When a light wave of a given frequency strikes a material with particles having the same or (resonant) vibrational frequencies, then those particles will absorb the energy of the light wave and transform it into thermal energy of vibrational motion. Since different atoms and molecules have different natural frequencies of vibration, they will selectively absorb different frequencies (or portions of the spectrum) of infrared light. Reflection and transmission of light waves occur because the frequencies of the light waves do not match the natural resonant frequencies of vibration of the objects. When infrared light of these frequencies strikes an object, the energy is reflected or transmitted.

If the object is transparent, then the light waves are passed on to neighboring atoms through the bulk of the material and re-emitted on the opposite side of the object. Such frequencies of light waves are said to be transmitted.

An object may be not transparent either because it reflects the incoming light or because it absorbs the incoming light. Almost all solids reflect a part and absorb a part of the incoming light.

When light falls onto a block of metal, it encounters atoms that are tightly packed in a regular lattice and a "sea of electrons" moving randomly between the atoms. In metals, most of these are non-bonding electrons (or free electrons) as opposed to the bonding electrons typically found in covalently bonded or ionically bonded non-metallic (insulating) solids. In a metallic bond, any potential bonding electrons can easily be lost by the atoms in a crystalline stucture. The effect of this delocalization is simply to exaggerate the effect of the 'sea of elctrons'. As a result of these electrons, most of the incoming light in metals is reflected back, which is why we see a shiny metal surface.

Most insulators (or dielectric materials) are held together by ionic bonds. Thus, these materials do not have free conduction electrons, and the bonding electrons reflect only a small fraction of the incident wave. The remaining frequencies (or wavelengths) are free to propagate (or be transmitted). This class of materials includes all ceramics and glasses.

If a dielectric material does not include light-absorbent additive molecules (pigments, dyes, colourants), it is usually transparent to the spectrum of visible light. Colour centres (or dye molecules, or 'dopants') in a dielectric absorb a portion of the incoming light wave. The remaining frequencies (or wavelengths) are free to be reflected or transmitted. This is how coloured glass is produced.

Most liquids and aqueous solutions are highly transparent. For example, water, cooking oil, rubbing alcohol, air, natural gas, are all clear. Absence of structural defects (voids, cracks, etc.) and molecular structure of most liquids are chiefly responsible for their excellent optical transmission. The ability of liquids to 'heal' internal defects via viscous flow is one of the reasons why some fibrous materials (e.g. paper or fabric) increase their apparent transparency when wetted. The liquid fills up numerous voids making the material more structurally homogeneous.

Light scattering in an ideal defect-free crystalline (non-metallic) solid which provides *no scattering centres* for incoming lightwaves will be due primarily to any effects of anharmonicity within the ordered lattice. Lightwave transmission will be highly directional due to the typical anisotropy of crystalline substances, which includes their symmetry group and Bravais lattice. For example, the seven different crystalline forms of quartz silica (silicon dioxide, SiO_2) are all clear, transparent materials.

Optically transparent materials focus on the response of a material to incoming light waves of a range of wavelengths. Guided light wave transmission via frequency selective waveguides involves the emerging field of fibre optics and the ability of certain glassy compositions as a transmission medium for a range of frequencies simultaneously (multimode optical fibre) with little or no interference between competing wavelengths or frequencies. This resonant mode of energy and data transmission via electromagnetic (light) wave propagation is relatively lossless.

An optical fibre is a cylindrical dielectric waveguide that transmits light along its axis by the process of total internal reflection. The fibre consists of a core surrounded by a cladding layer. To confine the optical signal in the core, the refractive index of the core must be greater than that of the cladding. The refractive index is the parameter reflecting the speed of light in a material. (Refractive index is the ratio of the speed of light in a vacuum to the speed of light in a given medium. The refractive index of a vacuum is therefore 1). The larger the refractive index, the more slowly light travels in that medium. Typical values for core and cladding of an optical fibre are 1.48 and 1.46, respectively.

When light traveling in a dense medium hits a boundary at a steep angle, the light will be completely reflected. This effect, called total internal reflection, is used in optical fibres to confine light in the core. Light travels along the fibre bouncing back and forth off of the boundary. Because the light must strike the boundary with an angle greater than the critical angle, only light that enters the fibre within a certain range of angles will be propagated. This range of angles is called the acceptance cone of the fibre. The size of this acceptance cone is a function of the refractive index difference between the fibre's core and cladding. Optical waveguides are used as components in integrated optical circuits (e.g. combined with lasers or light-emitting diodes, LEDs) or as the transmission medium in local and long haul optical communication systems.

Attenuation in fibre optics, also known as transmission loss, is the reduction in intensity of the light beam (or signal) with respect to distance traveled through a transmission medium. Attenuation coefficients in fibre optics usually use units of dB/km through the medium due to the relatively high quality of transparency of modern optical transmission media. The medium is usually a fibre of silica glass that confines the incident light beam to the inside. Attenuation is an important factor limiting the transmission of a signal across large distances. Thus, much research has gone into both limiting the attenuation and maximizing the amplification of the optical signal.

Attenuation is caused primarily by scattering and absorption. The scattering of light is caused by molecular level irregularities (compositional fluctuations) in the glass structure. This same phenomenon is seen as one of the limiting factors in the transparency of infrared missile domes.

Further attenuation is caused by light absorbed by residual materials, such as metals or water ions, within the fibre core and inner cladding. In optical fibre, light leakage due to bending, splices, connectors, or other outside forces are other factors resulting in attenuation.

Multi-phonon Absorption

The design of any optically transparent device requires the selection of materials based upon knowledge of their properties and limitations. The lattice absorption characteristics observed at the lower frequency regions (mid-infrared to far-infrared wavelength range) define the long-wavelength transparency limit of the material. They are the result of the interactive coupling between the motions of thermally induced vibrations of the constituent atoms and molecules of the solid lattice and the incident light wave radiation. Hence, all materials are bounded by limiting regions of absorption caused by atomic and molecular vibrations (bond-stretching)in the far-infrared spectral region (>10 μm).

The concepts of temperature and thermal equilibrium associated with ionic solids are based on individual atoms and molecules in the system possessing vibrational motion. The frequencies of the normal modes of a system are known as its natural frequencies or resonant frequencies. These thermal vibrational modes are associated with atomic and molecular displacements, producing both longitudinal and transverse waves of atomic and molecular displacement.

In the longitudinal (or acoustic) mode, the displacement of particles from their positions of equilibrium coincides with the propagation direction of the wave. Mechanical longitudinal waves have been also referred to as *compression waves*. For transverse (or optical) modes, individual particles move perpendicular to the propagation of the wave.

As the rules of quantum mechanics apply to all the different vibrational modes in the solid, the lattice pulsates as a complete assembly in discrete energy steps, or thermal phonons. A phonon is a quantized mode of vibration occurring in a rigid crystal lattice. The study of phonons is an important part of solid state physics, because phonons play a major role in many of the physical properties of solids, including a material's thermal and electrical conductivity.

The phonon is related to both the frequency of vibration and the temperature. If the temperature is raised, the amplitude of vibration increases. The concept of the phonon is therefore considered as the quantum of lattice vibrational energy onto which is superimposed a complex pattern of standing and/or traveling waves that represent changes in temperature. If the solid is at a uniform temperature, the standing wave concept is adequate as the phonon vibrations are uniformly distributed.

Multi-phonon absorption occurs when two or more phonons simultaneously interact to produce electric dipole moments with which the incident radiation may couple. These dipoles can absorb energy from the incident radiation, reaching a maximum coupling with the radiation when the frequency is equal to the vibrational mode of the molecular dipole (e.g. Si-O bond in quartz) in the far-infrared spectral region.

All of the resonant absorption processes involved in an optically transparent material can be explained by the same common principle. At particular frequencies, the incident radiation is allowed to propagate through the lattice producing the observed transparency. Other frequencies however, are forbidden when the incident radiation is at resonance with any of the properties of the lattice material (e.g. molecular vibrational frequencies), and as such are transferred as thermal energy, exciting the atoms or electrons.

In order that a mode of vibration can absorb, a mechanism for coupling the vibrational motion to the electromagnetic radiation must exist. Transfer of electromagnetic radiation from the incident medium to the material is in the form of a couple, where the lattice vibration produces an oscillating dipole moment which can be driven by the oscillating electric field of the light wave, or radiation. Thus, the energy absorbed from the light wave will be converted into vibrational motion of the molecules.

Light Scattering in Ceramics

Optical transparency in polycrystalline materials is limited by the amount of light which is scattered by their microstructural features. Light scattering depends on the wavelength of the light. Limits to spatial scales of visibility (using white light) therefore arise, depending on the frequency of the light wave and the physical dimension of the scattering centre. For example, since visible light has a wavelength scale on the order of a micrometer, scattering centres will have dimensions on a similar spatial scale. Primary scattering centres in polycrystalline materials include microstructural defects such as pores and grain boundaries. The volume fraction of microscopic pores has to be less than one per cent for high-quality optical transmission, that is the material density should be 99.99 per cent of the theoretical crystalline density. In addition to pores, most of the interfaces in a typical metal or ceramic object are in the form of grain boundaries which separate tiny regions of crystalline order. When the size of the scattering center (or grain boundary) is reduced below the size of the wavelength of the light being scattered, the scattering no longer occurs to any significant extent.

In the formation of polycrystalline materials (metals and ceramics) the size of the crystalline grains is determined largely by the size of the crystalline particles present in the raw material during formation (or pressing) of the object. Moreover, the size of the grain boundaries scales directly with particle size. Thus a reduction of the original particle size well below the wavelength of visible light (about 1/15 of the light wavelength or roughly 600/15 = 40 nm) eliminates much of light scattering, resulting in a translucent or even transparent material.

Computer modelling of light transmission through translucent ceramic alumina has shown that microscopic pores trapped near grain boundaries cause act as primary scattering centres. The volume fraction of porosity had to be reduced below one per cent for high-quality optical transmission (99.99% of theoretical density). This goal has been readily accomplished and amply demonstrated in laboratories and research facilities worldwide using the emerging chemical processing methods encompassed by the methods of sol-gel chemistry and nanotechnology.

Applications

Transparent ceramics have recently acquired a high degree of interest and notoriety, the basic applications being high energy lasers, transparent armor windows, nose cones for heat seeking missiles, radiation detectors for non-destructive testing, high energy physics, space exploration, security and medical imaging applications.

The development of transparent panel products will have other potential advanced applications including high strength, impact-resistant materials that can be used for domestic windows and skylights. Perhaps more important is that walls and other applications will have improved overall strength, especially for high-shear conditions found in high seismic and wind exposures. If the expected improvements in mechanical properties bear out, the traditional limits seen on glazing areas in today's building codes could quickly become outdated if the window area actually contributes to the shear resistance of the wall.

Currently available infrared transparent materials typically exhibit a trade-off between optical performance, mechanical strength and price. For example, sapphire (crystalline alumina) is very strong, but it is expensive and lacks full transparency throughout the 3-5 micrometre mid-infrared range. Yttria is fully transparent from 3-5 micrometres, but lacks sufficient strength, hardness, and thermal shock resistance for high-performance aerospace applications. Not surprisingly, a combination of these two materials in the form of the yttrium aluminium garnet (YAG) is one of the top performers in the field.

21

Fibreglass

Fibreglass, (also called fibreglass and glass fibre), is material made from extremely fine fibres of glass. It is used as a reinforcing agent for many polymer products; the resulting composite material, properly known as fibre-reinforced polymer (FRP) or glass-reinforced plastic (GRP), is called 'fibreglass' in popular usage. Glassmakers throughout history have experimented with glass fibres, but mass manufacture of fibreglass was only made possible with the invention of finer machine tooling. In 1893, Edward Drummond Libbey exhibited a dress at the World's Columbian Exposition incorporating glass fibres with the diameter and texture of silk fibres. This was first worn by the popular stage actress of the time Georgia Cayvan.

What is commonly known as 'fibreglass' today, however, was invented in 1938 by Russell Games Slayter of Owens-Corning as a material to be used as insulation. It is marketed under the trade name Fibreglass, which has become a genericized trademark. A somewhat similar, but more expensive technology used for applications requiring very high strength and low weight is the use of carbon fibre.

Glass fibre is formed when thin strands of silica-based or other formulation glass is extruded into many fibres with small diametres suitable for textile processing. The technique of heating and drawing glass into fine fibres has been known for millennia; however, the use of these fibres for textile applications is more recent. Until this time all fibreglass had been manufactured as staple (a term used to describe naturally formed clusters or locks of wool fibres). The first commercial production of fibreglass was in 1936. In 1938 Owens-Illinois Glass Company and Corning Glass Works joined to form the Owens-Corning Fibreglass Corporation. When the two companies joined to produce and promote fibreglass, they introduced continuous filament glass fibres. Owens-Corning is still the major fibreglass producer in the market today.

The types of fibreglass most commonly used are mainly E-glass (alumino-borosilicate glass with less than 1 wt% alkali oxides, mainly used for glass-reinforced plastics), but also A-glass (alkali-lime glass with little or no boron oxide), E-CR-glass (alumino-lime silicate with less than 1 wt% alkali oxides, has high acid resistance), C-glass (alkali-lime glass with high boron oxide content, used for example for glass staple fibres), D-glass (borosilicate glass with high dielectric constant), R-glass (alumino silicate glass without MgO and CaO with high mechanical requirements), and S-glass (alumino silicate glass without CaO but with high MgO content with high tensile strength).

Chemistry

The basis of textile-grade glass fibres is silica, SiO_2. In its pure form it exists as a polymer, $(SiO_2)_n$. It has no true melting point but softens at 2,000°C (3,630°F), where it starts to degrade. At 1,713°C (3,115°F), most of the molecules can move about freely. If the glass is then cooled quickly, they will be unable to form an ordered structure. In the polymer, it forms SiO_4 groups which are configured as a tetrahedron with the silicon atom at the center and four oxygen atoms at the corners. These atoms then form a network bonded at the corners by sharing the oxygen atoms.

The vitreous and crystalline states of silica (glass and quartz) have similar energy levels on a molecular basis, also implying that the glassy form is extremely stable. In order to induce crystallization, it must be heated to temperatures above 1,200°C (2,190°F) for long periods of time.

Although pure silica is a perfectly viable glass and glass fibre, it must be worked with at very high temperatures, which is a drawback unless its specific chemical properties are needed. It is usual to introduce impurities into the glass in the form of other materials to lower its working temperature. These materials also impart various other properties to the glass which may be beneficial in different applications. The first type of glass used for fibre was soda lime glass or A glass. It was not very resistant to alkali. A new type, E-glass, was formed; this is an alumino-borosilicate glass that is alkali free (<2%). This was the first glass formulation used for continuous filament formation. E-glass still makes up most of the fibreglass production in the world. Its particular components may differ slightly in percentage, but must fall within a specific range. The letter E is used because it was originally for electrical applications. S-glass is a high-strength formulation for use when tensile strength is the most important property. C-glass was developed to resist attack from chemicals, mostly acids which destroy E-glass. T-glass is a North American variant of C-glass. A-glass is an industry term for cullet glass, often bottles, made into fibre. AR-glass is alkali-resistant glass. Most glass fibres have limited solubility in water but are very dependent on pH. Chloride ions will also attack and dissolve E-glass surfaces.

Since E-glass does not really melt, but soften, the softening point is defined as "the temperature at which a 0.55-0.77 mm diametre fibre 235 mm long, elongates under its own weight at 1 mm/min when suspended vertically and heated at the rate of 5°C per minute". The strain point is reached when the glass has a viscosity of $10^{14.5}$ poise. The annealing point, which is the temperature where the internal stresses are reduced to an acceptable commercial limit in 15 minutes, is marked by a viscosity of 10^{13} poise.

Properties

Glass fibres are useful because of their high ratio of surface area to weight. However, the increased surface area makes them much more susceptible to chemical attack. By trapping air within them, blocks of glass fibre make good thermal insulation, with a thermal conductivity of the order of 0.05 W/(m·K).

The strength of glass is usually tested and reported for 'virgin' or pristine fibres — those which have just been manufactured. The freshest, thinnest fibres are the strongest because the thinner fibres are more ductile. The more the surface is scratched, the less the resulting tenacity. Because glass has an amorphous structure, its properties are the same along the fibre and across the fibre. Humidity is an important factor in the tensile strength. Moisture is easily adsorbed, and can worsen microscopic cracks and surface defects, and lessen tenacity.

In contrast to carbon fibre, glass can undergo more elongation before it breaks. There is a correlation between bending diametre of the filament and the filament diametre. The viscosity of the molten glass is very important for manufacturing success. During drawing (pulling of the glass to reduce fibre circumference), the viscosity should be relatively low. If it is too high, the fibre will break during drawing. However, if it is too low, the glass will form droplets rather than drawing out into fibre.

Safety

Fibreglass has increased in popularity since the the discovery that asbestos causes cancer and its subsequent removal from most products. However, the safety of fibreglass is also being called into question, as research shows that the composition of this material (asbestos and fibreglass are both silicate fibres) causes similar toxicity as asbestos.

1970s studies on rats found that fibrous glass of less than 3 micrometres in diametre and greater than 20 micrometres in length is a 'potent carcinogen'. Likewise, the International Agency for Research on Cancer found it "may reasonably be anticipated to be a carcinogen" in 1990. The American Conference of Governmental Industrial Hygienists, on the other hand, says that there is insufficient evidence, and that fibreglass is in group A4: "Not classifiable as a human carcinogen".

The North American Insulation Manufacturers Association (NAIMA) claims that fibreglass is fundamentally different from asbestos, since it is man-made instead of naturally-occurring. They claim that fibreglass "dissolves in the lungs", while asbestos remains in the body for life. Although both fibreglass and asbestos are made from silica filaments, NAIMA claims that asbestos is more dangerous because of its crystalline structure, which causes it to cleave into smaller, more dangerous pieces, citing the U.S. Department of Health and Human Services.

Synthetic vitreous fibres differ from asbestos in two ways that may provide at least partial explanations for their lower toxicity. Because most synthetic vitreous fibres are not crystalline like asbestos, they do not split longitudinally to form thinner fibres. They also generally have markedly less biopersistence in biological tissues than asbestos fibres because they can undergo dissolution and transverse breakage.

A 1998 rat study found that the biopersistence of synthetic fibres after one year was 0.04-10 per cent, but 27 per cent for amosite asbestos. Fibres that persisted longer were found to be more carcinogenic.

Glass-reinforced Plastic

Glass-reinforced plastic (GRP) is a composite material or fibre-reinforced plastic made of a plastic reinforced by fine glass fibres. Like graphite-reinforced plastic, the composite material is commonly referred to by the name of its reinforcing fibres (fibreglass). Thermosetting plastics are normally used for GRP production — most often unsaturated polyester (using 2-butanone peroxide aka MEK peroxide as a catalyst), but vinylester or epoxy are also used. Traditionally, styrene monomer was used as a reactive diluent in the resin formulation giving the resin a characteristic odour. More recently alternatives have been developed. The glass can be in the form of a chopped strand mat (CSM) or a woven fabric.

As with many other composite materials (such as reinforced concrete), the two materials act together, each overcoming the deficits of the other. Whereas the plastic resins are strong in compressive loading and relatively weak in tensile strength, the glass fibres are very strong in tension but have no strength against compression. By combining the two materials, GRP becomes a material that resists both compressive and tensile forces well. The two materials may be used uniformly or the glass may be specifically placed in those portions of the structure that will experience tensile loads.

Uses for regular fibreglass include mats, thermal insulation, electrical insulation, reinforcement of various materials, tent poles, sound absorption, heat- and corrosion-resistant fabrics, high-strength fabrics, pole vault poles, arrows, bows and crossbows, translucent roofing panels, automobile bodies, hockey sticks, surfboards, boat hulls, and paper honeycomb. It has been used for medical purposes in casts. Fibreglass is extensively used for making FRP tanks and vessels. Fibreglass is also used in the design of Irish stepdance shoes.

In the 1986-1987 America's Cup, New Zealand, with the help of Rene Felcher, Bruce Farr, and Michael Fay, entered a boat whose hull was made of the lighter fibreglass, nicknamed the 'Plastic Fantastic', and given the call sign KZ7. This caused a similar controversy and protests as those generated four years earlier by Australia's used of winged keels as designed by the now late Ben Lexcen. United States sailor Dennis Conner was particularly critical of both new innovations in their time. The boats proved fast on occasion, being much lighter than the standard models, even those with winged keels, but the experience of Conner allowed him to return the World's oldest sporting trophy to the United States.

It is the most commonly used home insulating material in the United States, though it is one of the most ineffective. Fibreglass makes a great insulating material until outside temperatures drops below 68 degrees Fahrenheit. In fact at 35 degrees Fahrenheit, it loses aproximately 75 per cent of its R-value.

Role of Recycling in Fibreglass Manufacturing

Manufacturers of fibreglass insulation can use recycled glass. Owens Corning's fibreglass has 40 per cent recycled glass. A recycling programme begun in 2009 in Kansas City, Kansas, will ship crushed recycled glass, called cullet, to the Owens Corning plant that will use it as raw material for fibreglass making.

22

Composite Material

Composite materials (or *composites* for short) are Engineered materials made from two or more constituent materials with significantly different physical or chemical properties which remain separate and distinct on a macroscopic level within the finished structure.

History

Wood is a natural composite of cellulose fibres in a matrix of lignin. The most primitive man-made composite materials were straw and mud combined to form bricks for building construction; the Biblical Book of Exodus speaks of the Israelites being oppressed by Pharaoh, by being forced to make bricks without straw being provided. The ancient brick-making process can still be seen on Egyptian tomb paintings in the Metropolitan Museum of Art. The most advanced examples perform routinely on spacecraft in demanding environments. The most visible applications pave our roadways in the form of either steel and aggregate reinforced portland cement or asphalt concrete. Those composites closest to our personal hygiene form our shower stalls and bath tubs made of fibreglass. Solid surface, imitation granite and cultured marble sinks and counter tops are widely used to enhance our living experiences.

Composites are made up of individual materials referred to as constituent materials. There are two categories of constituent materials: matrix and reinforcement. At least one portion of each type is required. The matrix material surrounds and supports the reinforcement materials by maintaining their relative positions. The reinforcements impart their special mechanical and physical properties to enhance the matrix properties. A synergism produces material properties unavailable from the individual constituent materials, while the wide variety of matrix and strengthening materials allows the designer of the product or structure to choose an optimum combination.

Engineered composite materials must be formed to shape. The matrix material can be introduced to the reinforcement before or after the reinforcement material is placed into the mold cavity or onto the mold surface. The matrix material experiences a melding event, after which the part shape is essentially set. Depending upon the nature of the matrix material, this melding event can occur in various ways such as chemical polymerization or solidification from the melted state.

A variety of molding methods can be used according to the end-item design requirements. The principal factors impacting the methodology are the natures of the chosen matrix and reinforcement materials. Another important factor is the gross quantity of material to be produced. Large quantities can be used to justify high capital expenditures for rapid and automated manufacturing technology. Small production quantities are accommodated with lower capital expenditures but higher labour and tooling costs at a correspondingly slower rate.

Most commercially produced composites use a polymer matrix material often called a resin solution. There are many different polymers available depending upon the starting raw ingredients. There are several broad categories, each with numerous variations. The most common are known as polyester, vinyl ester, epoxy, phenolic, polyimide, polyamide, polypropylene, PEEK, and others. The reinforcement materials are often fibres but also commonly ground minerals. The various methods described below have been developed to reduce the resin content of the final product, or the fibre content is increased. As a rule of thumb, lay up results in a product containing 60 per cent resin and 40 per cent fibre, whereas vacuum infusion gives a final product with 40 per cent resin and 60 per cent fibre content. The strength of the product is greatly dependent on this ratio.

Moulding Methods

In general, the reinforcing and matrix materials are combined, compacted and processed to undergo a melding event. After the melding event, the part shape is essentially set, although it can deform under certain process conditions. For a thermoset polymeric matrix material, the melding event is a curing reaction that is initiated by the application of additional heat or chemical reactivity such as an organic peroxide. For a thermoplastic polymeric matrix material, the melding event is a solidification from the melted state. For a metal matrix material such as titanium foil, the melding event is a fusing at high pressure and a temperature near the melt point.

For many molding methods, it is convenient to refer to one mold piece as a 'lower' mold and another mold piece as an 'upper' mold. Lower and upper refer to the different faces of the molded panel, not the mold's configuration in space. In this convention, there is always a lower mold, and sometimes an upper mold. Part construction begins by applying materials to the lower mold. Lower mold and upper mold are more generalized descriptors than more common and specific terms such as male side, female side, a-side, b-side, tool side, bowl, hat, mandrel, etc. Continuous manufacturing processes use a different nomenclature.

The molded product is often referred to as a panel. For certain geometries and material combinations, it can be referred to as a casting. For certain continuous processes, it can be referred to as a profile. Applied with a pressure roller, a spray device or manually. This process is generally done at ambient temperature and atmospheric pressure. Two variations of open moulding are Hand Layup and Spray-up.

Vacuum Bag Moulding

A process using a two-sided mould set that shapes both surfaces of the panel. On the lower side is a rigid mould and on the upper side is a flexible membrane or vacuum bag. The flexible membrane can be a reusable silicone material or an extruded polymer film. Then, vacuum is applied to the mould cavity. This process can be performed at either ambient or elevated temperature with ambient atmospheric pressure acting upon the vacuum bag. Most economical way is using a venturi vacuum and air compressor or a vacuum pump.

Pressure Bag Moulding

This process is related to vacuum bag moulding in exactly the same way as it sounds. A solid female mould is used along with a flexible male mould. The reinforcement is placed inside the female mould with just enough resin to allow the fabric to stick in place. A measured amount of resin is then liberally brushed indiscriminately into the mould and the mould is then clamped to a machine that contains the male flexible mould. The flexible male membrane is then inflated with heated compressed air or possibly steam. The female mould can also be heated. Excess resin is forced out along with trapped air. This process is extensively used in the production of composite helmets due to the lower cost of unskilled labour. Cycle times for a helmet bag moulding machine vary from 20 to 45 minutes, but the finished shells require no further curing if the moulds are heated.

Autoclave Moulding

A process using a two-sided mold set that forms both surfaces of the panel. On the lower side is a rigid mold and on the upper side is a flexible membrane made from silicone or an extruded polymer film such as nylon. Reinforcement materials can be placed manually or robotically. They include continuous fibre forms fashioned into textile constructions. Most often, they are pre-impregnated with the resin in the form of prepreg fabrics or unidirectional tapes. In some instances, a resin film is placed upon the lower mold and dry reinforcement is placed above. The upper mold is installed and vacuum is applied to the mold cavity. The assembly is placed into an autoclave. This process is generally performed at both elevated pressure and elevated temperature. The use of elevated pressure facilitates a high fibre volume fraction and low void content for maximum structural efficiency.

Resin Transfer Moulding (RTM)

A process using a two-sided mould set that forms both surfaces of the panel. The lower side is a rigid mould. The upper side can be a rigid or flexible mould. Flexible moulds can be made from composite materials, silicone or extruded polymer films such as nylon. The two sides fit together to produce a mould cavity. The distinguishing feature of resin transfer moulding is that the reinforcement materials are placed into this cavity and the mould set is closed prior to the introduction of matrix material. Resin transfer moulding includes numerous varieties which differ in the mechanics of how the resin is introduced to the reinforcement in the mould cavity. These variations include everything from vacuum infusion (for resin infusion see also boat building) to vacuum assisted resin transfer moulding (VARTM). This process can be performed at either ambient or elevated temperature.

Other types of molding include press molding, transfer molding, pultrusion molding, filament winding, casting, centrifugal casting and continuous casting. There are also forming capabilities including CNC filament winding, vacuum infusion, wet lay-up, compression molding, and thermoplastic molding, to name a few. The use of curing ovens and paint booths is also needed for some projects.

Tooling

Some types of tooling materials used in the manufacturing of composites structures include invar, steel, aluminum, reinforced silicone rubber, nickel, and carbon fibre. Selection of the tooling material is typically based on, but not limited to, the coefficient of thermal expansion, expected number of cycles, end item tolerance, desired or required surface condition, method of cure, glass transition temperature of the material being molded, molding method, matrix, cost and a variety of other considerations.

Properties

Mechanics

The physical properties of composite materials are generally not isotropic (independent of direction of applied force) in nature, but rather are typically orthotropic (different depending on the direction of the applied force or load). For instance, the stiffness of a composite panel will often depend upon the orientation of the applied forces and/or moments. Panel stiffness is also dependent on the design of the panel. For instance, the fibre reinforcement and matrix used, the method of panel build, thermoset versus thermoplastic, type of weave, and orientation of fibre axis to the primary force.

In contrast, isotropic materials (for example, aluminium or steel), in standard wrought forms, typically have the same stiffness regardless of the directional orientation of the applied forces and/or moments.

The relationship between forces/moments and strains/curvatures for an isotropic material can be described with the following material properties: Young's Modulus, the Shear Modulus and the Poisson's ratio, in relatively simple mathematical relationships. For the anisotropic material, it requires the mathematics of a second order tensor and up to 21 material property constants. For the special case of orthogonal isotropy, there are three different material property constants for each of Young's Modulus, Shear Modulus and Poisson's ratio–a total of 9 constants to describe the relationship between forces/moments and strains/ curvatures.

Techniques that take advantage of the anistropic properties of the materials include mortise and tenon joints (in natural composites such as wood) and Pi Joints in synthetic composites.

Resins

Typically, most common composite materials, including fibreglass, carbon fibre, and Kevlar, include at least two parts, the substrate and the resin.

Polyester resin, tends to have yellowish tint, and is suitable for most backyard projects. Its weaknesses are that it is UV sensitive and can tend to degrade over time, and thus generally is also coated to help preserve it. It is often used in the making of surfboards and for marine applications. Its hardener is a MEKP, and is mixed at 14 drops per oz. MEKP is composed of methyl ethyl ketone peroxide, a catalyst. When MEKP is mixed with the resin, the resulting chemical reaction causes heat to build up and cure or harden the resin.

Vinylester resin, tends to have a purplish to bluish to greenish tint. This resin has lower viscosity than polyester resin, and is more transparent. This resin is often billed as being fuel resistant, but will melt in contact with gasoline. This resin tends to be more resistant over time to degradation than polyester resin, and is more flexible. It uses the same hardener as polyester resin (at the same mix ratio) and the cost is approximately the same.

Epoxy resin is almost totally transparent when cured. In the aerospace industry, epoxy is used as a structural matrix material or as a structural glue.

Shape memory polymer (SMP) resins have varying visual characteristics depending on their formulation. These resins may be epoxy-based, which can be used for auto body and outdoor equipment repairs; cyanate-ester-based, which are used in space applications; and acrylate-based, which can be used in very cold temperature applications, such as for sensors that indicate whether perishable goods have warmed above a certain maximum temperature. These resins are unique in that their shape can be repeatedly changed by heating above their glass transition temperature (T_g). When heated, they become flexible and elastic, allowing for easy configuration. Once they are cooled, they will maintain their new shape. The resins will return to their original shapes when they are reheated above their T_g. The advantage of shape memory polymer resins is that they can be shaped and reshaped repeatedly without losing their material properties, and these resins can be used in fabricating shape memory composites.

Categories of Fibre-reinforced Composite Materials

Fibre-reinforced composite materials can be divided into two main categories normally referred to as short fibre-reinforced materials and continuous fibre-reinforced materials. Continuous reinforced materials will often constitute a layered or laminated structure. The woven and continuous fibre styles are typically available in a variety of forms, being pre-impregnated with the given matrix (resin), dry, uni-directional tapes of various widths, plain weave, harness satins, braided, and stitched.

The short and long fibres are typically employed in compression molding and sheet molding operations. These come in the form of flakes, chips, and random mate (which can also be made from a continuous fibre laid in random fashion until the desired thickness of the ply/laminate is achieved).

Failure

Shock, impact, or repeated cyclic stresses can cause the laminate to separate at the interface between two layers, a condition known as delamination. Individual fibres can separate from the matrix e.g. fibre pull-out.

Composites can fail on the microscopic or macroscopic scale. Compression failures can occur at both the macro scale or at each individual reinforcing fibre in compression buckling. Tension failures can be net section failures of the part or degradation of the composite at a microscopic scale where one or more of the layers in the composite fail in tension of the matrix or failure the bond between the matrix and fibres.

Some composites are brittle and have little reserve strength beyond the initial onset of failure while others may have large deformations and have reserve energy absorbing capacity past the onset of damage. The variations in fibres and matrices that are available and the mixtures that can be made with blends leave a very broad range of properties that can be designed into a composite structure. The best known failure of a brittle ceramic matrix composite occurred when the carbon-carbon composite tile on the leading edge of the wing of the Space Shuttle Columbia fractured when impacted during take-off. It led to catastrophic break-up of the vehicle when it re-entered the Earth's atmosphere on February 1, 2003.

Compared to metals, composites have relatively poor bearing strength.

To aid in predicting and preventing failures, composites are tested before and after construction. Pre-construction testing may use finite element analysis (FEA) for ply-by-ply analysis of curved surfaces and predicting wrinkling, crimping and dimpling of composites. Materials may be tested after construction through several non-destructive methods including ultrasonics, thermography, shearography and X-ray radiography.

Examples

Materials

Fibre-reinforced polymers or FRPs include wood (comprising cellulose fibres in a lignin and hemicellulose matrix), carbon-fibre reinforced plastic or CFRP, and glass-reinforced plastic or GRP. If classified by matrix then there are thermoplastic composites, short fibre thermoplastics, long fibre thermoplastics or long fibre-reinforced thermoplastics. There are numerous thermoset composites, but advanced systems usually incorporate aramid fibre and carbon fibre in an epoxy resin matrix.

Shape memory polymer composites are high-performance composites, formulated using fibre or fabric reinforcement and shape memory polymer resin as the matrix. Since a shape memory polymer resin is used as the matrix, these composites have the ability to be easily manipulated into various configurations when they are heated above their activation temperatures and will exhibit high strength and stiffness at lower temperatures. They can also be reheated and reshaped repeatedly without losing their material properties. These composites are ideal for applications such as lightweight, rigid, deployable structures; rapid manufacturing; and dynamic reinforcement.

Composites can also use metal fibres reinforcing other metals, as in metal matrix composites or MMC. Magnesium is often used in MMCs because it has similar mechanical properties as epoxy. The benefit of magnesium is that it does not degrade in outer space. Ceramic matrix composites include bone (hydroxyapatite reinforced with collagen fibres), Cermet (ceramic and metal) and concrete. Ceramic matrix composites are built primarily for toughness, not for strength. Organic matrix/ceramic aggregate composites include asphalt concrete, mastic asphalt, mastic roller hybrid, dental composite, syntactic foam and mother of pearl. Chobham armour is a special type of composite armour used in military applications.

Additionally, thermoplastic composite materials can be formulated with specific metal powders resulting in materials with a density range from 2 g/cm^3 to 11 g/cm^3 (same density as lead). The most common name for this type of material is High Gravity Compound (HGC), although Lead

Replacement is also used. These materials can be used in place of traditional materials such as aluminum, stainless steel, brass, bronze, copper, lead, and even tungsten in weighting, balancing (for example, modifying the centre of gravity of a tennis racquet), vibration dampening, and radiation shielding applications. High density composites are an economically viable option when certain materials are deemed hazardous and are banned (such as lead) or when secondary operations costs (such as machining, finishing, or coating) are a factor.

Engineered wood includes a wide variety of different products such as plywood, oriented strand board, wood plastic composite (recycled wood fibre in polyethylene matrix), Pykrete (sawdust in ice matrix), Plastic-impregnated or laminated paper or textiles, Arborite, Formica (plastic) and Micarta. Other engineered laminate composites, such as Mallite, use a central core of end grain balsa wood, bonded to surface skins of light alloy or GRP. These generate low-weight, high rigidity materials.

Products

Composite materials have gained popularity (despite their generally high cost) in high-performance products that need to be lightweight, yet strong enough to take harsh loading conditions such as aerospace components (tails, wings, fuselages, propellers), boat and scull hulls, bicycle frames and racing car bodies . Other uses include fishing rods, storage tanks, and baseball bats. The new Boeing 787 structure including the wings and fuselage is composed largely of composites. Composite materials are also becoming more common in the realm of orthopaedic surgery.

Carbon composite is a key material in today's launch vehicles and spacecraft. It is widely used in solar panel substrates, antenna reflectors and yokes of spacecraft. It is also used in payload adapters, inter-stage structures and heat shields of launch vehicles.

In 2007 an all-composite military High Mobility Multi-purpose Wheeled Vehicle (HMMWV or Hummvee) was introduced by TPI Composites Inc and Armor Holdings Inc, the first all-composite military vehicle. By using composites the vehicle is lighter, allowing higher payloads. In 2008 carbon fibre and DuPont Kevlar (five times stronger than steel) were combined with enhanced thermoset resins to make military transit cases by ECS Composites creating 30 per cent lighter cases with high strength.

23

Strength of Glass

Fibres constitute a major component of the glass industry. The traditional fibreglass companies manufacture either reinforcement fibres or fibres for thermal and acoustic insulations. During the last three or four decades, a new glass fibre industry, namely the fibre optics industry, has seen explosive growth based on the use of silica glass fibres as optical waveguides. In particular, Dr. Robert D. Maurer has been recognized for his creative role in the development of fibre optics for telecommunications and guided lightwave technology for creating transparent materials with capabilities in the UV-Vis-IR portions of the electromagnetic spectrum. These applications require high tensile strengths over periods of time exceeding as much as 20 years. Consequently, there has arisen a great interest in quantifying the strength of glass and much has been documented and reviewed in the established literature.

Thus, silica-based optical fibres have been successfully implemented in spite of their limited mechanical properties as brittle materials. E.G. Current methods are used to produce long lengths (tens of kilometres) of these fibres that are drawn and coated in-line. The preform and drawing procedures allow the production of fibre that is free of flaws on the surface, thus exhibiting essentially theoretical strength under typical loading conditions (~5.5 GPa). The few defects that occur in manufacturing are eliminated by a proof-testing method which allows the remaining length of fibre to acquire virtually any desired level of strength. While the commonly specified proof stress is approximately 700 MPa, By reducing the available continuous lengths and increasing the sophistication of the procedure, proof stresses in excess of 700 MPa are possible.

This level of success does not apply to all classes of fibre materials. And while their capabilities can sometimes be more or less predicted, there is much less data available on multicomponent silicate fibres, hollow waveguides, and photonic crystal guides. The mechanical properties of other specialty glass fibres, such as heavy metal fluoride (HMF), telluride, phosphate and chalcogenide glasses, have also been studied with a wide range of results.

Strength Types

The strength of freshly manufactured fibres can be classified as intrinsic or extrinsic, and as inert or fatigue. For improved mechanical reliability and increased production, the primary factor is the extrinsic fatigue strength. Alternaitvely, for a fundamental understanding of strength in terms of microstructure, one is more concerned with the intrinsic inert strength, and how it changes with chemical composition.

Much remains unknown about both the extrinsic and the intrinsic strengths. For the extrinsic strengths, this relates mostly to the identity of the flaws and the role of crack nucleation around inclusions. The difficulty in studying large extrinsic flaws lies in the fact that they occur very infrequently (maybe one flaw in hundreds of kilometers of fibre).

Glass fibres are produced routinely with strengths which are more than adequate for their intended use.In recent years, research has shifted to studying how to improve production efficiencies by eliminating the sources of low strength fibres. However, there is still ongoing research in the strength of glass fibres for two reasons.

For starters, the strength of pristine fibres is the *intrinsic* strength of a glass composition. Intrinsic strength refers to strength of a glass containing no flaws either in the bulk or on the surface and is determined by the chemical composition and molecular structure of a glass over a range of spatial scales. However, understanding of intrinsic strength is still unsatisfactory and much is still unknown.

Secondly, pristine fibres exhibit fatigue much like fibres containing microcracks. However, the mechanisms of fatigue in the absence of cracks are not well understood at present. Strength of a glass fibre depends on the way it is measured. In other words, the measured strength is a function of testing variables such as the type of test (pure tension or bend test), the strain rate used, and the relative humidity and the temperature of the testing environment. The testing parameters influence the measured value of the strength because of a stress-enhanced environment-induced phenomenon known as fatigue. Strength measured in the absence of fatigue is called inert strength. Fatigue causes the strength of a glass sample to degrade with time in the presence of stress.

Because of fatigue, failure can occur after a sufficiently long time at values of stress much less than the inert strength. The mechanism of fatigue in glasses containing cracks is reasonably well understood. It occurs as a result of a chemical reaction between adsorbed water and the stressed siloxane bond at the crack tip leading to slow growth of the crack length.

Interestingly, pristine fibres also exhibit fatigue which is qualitatively similar to fatigue in fibres with cracks. However, as stated previously, the mechanism of fatigue in the absence of cracks is not clear at present. Such an understanding is required for the estimation of the life times of fibres under low levels of stress. The purpose of this article is to provide an overview of the fundamental understanding of the strength of bare glass fibres.

The fundamental concepts of glass fibre strength are summarized here in addition to an introduction to the most comon terms used to describe it in the literature. The main subjects are as follows:

- Extrinsic inert strength
- Extrinsic fatigue strength
- Intrinsic inert strength
- Intrinsic fatigue strength

The subject of extrinsic strength precedes the discussion of intrinsic strength, as it is generally more thoroughly understood.

Griffith Defects

Alan Arnold Griffith established that the strength of glass is largely determined by surface defects and cracks of various shapes and depths, which arise mainly from contact with solids and from defects in the silica blanks or fibre preforms. An external stress S results in stress concentrations at the ends of the surface defects, which are proportional to the external load mulitplied by the square root of the ratio of the crack depth 'd' to the radius at the end of the flaw (or defect) 'r'.

When these stresses become equal to or greater than the chemical binding forces between the atoms, the material fails. These Griffith defects (or flaws) are typically on the order of size range (or spatial scale) as the micron (1 μm). The defects and cracks are distributed randomly along the length of the fibre, so the strengths of limited segments can vary considerably. Thus, the strength is to be considered as a random quantity. The strength distribution as function of load largely characterizes the level of preparation of the fibres as well as the condition of the blanks or fibre preforms. A distinction can be drawn between the static strength and the dynamic strength or fatigue resistance.

A flaw is an extrinsic defect in a glass. Common examples of (3-dimensional) flaws are scratches, indents, inclusions, devitrified regions, and bubbles. One often speaks of 'intrinsic flaws' when referring to the intrinsic inhomogeneities present in a glass. Examples of intrinsic inhomogeneities are point defects, structural inhomogeneities caused by frozen-in density and composition fluctuations, and nanoscale roughness on glass surface. The term 'flaw' is used in this article specifically to indicate extrinsic flaws.

A crack is a 2-dimensional flaw — an area across which the bonds are broken. The boundary of this area is called the crack tip. The curvature (normal to the plane of the crack) at the tip is assumed to be infinitely sharp in the continuum models but is of atomistic dimensions in real materials. The detailed atomistic structure of a crack tip is unresolved at present. However, it may be of use to note that in silicate glasses, a crack tip has a radius of curvature on the order of 0.3 nm which is approximately the size of a single siloxane bridge [-Si-O-Si-].

Under the application of a tensile stress, 3-dimensional flaws (e.g., pores and inclusions) cannot grow. Only cracks can grow under tensile stress. Sometimes one speaks of the 'growth of a flaw' (not a crack), implying the growth of a microcrack nucleated at or near that flaw. It is clear that, when a material does not have a pre-existing crack, a crack must nucleate at some moment of time prior to fracture.

Weibull Statistics

Measured strengths of identically prepared glass fibres always shown a wide statisitical distribution. It is customary to plot the measured strength distribution on a Weibull plot where the ordinate is ln{ln [1/(1 - P)]] and the abscissa is ln S. Here P (S) is the cumulative probability of failure for strengths less than or equal to S. When measured strength values fall on a straight line (with slope m), the data imply a (unimodal) Weibull distribution of strengths given by the following:

$$P(S) = 1 - \exp[-(S/S_R)^m]$$

Here S_R is a scaling parameter which is related to the average strength, and the variable 'm' is called the 'Weibull modulus'. The Weibull distribution is that typically used for purposes of failure analysis in the design of high performance brittle materials such as glasses and ceramics. In general, a higher value of the Weibull modulus m implies a tighter statistical distribution (lesser spread) of the data.

Forensic inquiry into the failed process or product is often the starting point of failure analysis. Such inquiry is conducted using scientific analytical methods such as electrical and mechanical measurements, or by analysing failure data such as product reject reports or examples of previous failures of the same kind. The methods of forensic engineering are especially valuable in tracing product defects and flaws. They may include fatigue cracks, brittle cracks produced by stress corrosion cracking or environmental stress cracking.

Intrinsic Strength

When there are no flaws present, the measured strengths are called intrinsic. The strength of pristine fibres therefore provides the intrinsic strength of a glass composition. The intrinsic strength is denoted by S'. Intrinsic strengths are obtained when the following conditions are satisfied:

- Measured strength is constant with respect to the fibre diameter and length.
- Measured strengths are amongst the highest ones measured (typically > E/20, where E = Young's modulus of elasticity.)

Pristine Fibres

Fibres without flaws are called pristine or 'flawless'. Fibres with flaws are called nonpristine. Routinely manufactured fibres are generally non-pristine. Measuring the strength of pristine fibres experimentally can be quite tedious. It requires a careful preparation of the starting materials to ensure that they are free of flaws, careful forming of fibres in ultra-clean environments, capturing bare fibre samples before they come in contact with any other surface (such as the coating applicator or the collection drum), and testing of a large number of small fibre lengths immediately after capture with minimum additional handling.

Even after all these precautions, it is often not easy to establish whether pristine fibre strengths are being measured in an experiment. This is usually accomplished by accumulating data over many experiments as a function of several experimental parameters and making sure that the measured strengths are amongst the highest ones measured and are reproducible.

Because the probability of the existence of an extrinsic flaw increases with volume (or with total surface of test samples), intrinsic strength measurements require fibre samples of as small a diameter and as small a length as possible. The two-point bend technique offers the simplest way of carrying out such experiments — provided that the fibre is not too thin (diameter > 50 μm). This technique is routinely used for testing silica fibres (diametre ~ 125 μm). For smaller diameter glass fibres (5-20 μm), testing in pure tension is the only method available at present for measuring the intrinsic strength of a given glass composition.

Glass fibres have also become very important as load carrying components in fibre/matrix composites as high performance mechanical components in both the private end military sectors. Within this context, a loop test has been developed for testing the intrinsic bending strength of a glass fibre. By creating a loop in the fibre, and pulling on both ends, the radius of curvature of the loop decreases and eventually the fibre breaks due to bending.

Extrinsic Strength

Flaw-controlled strengths are called extrinsic. The strengths of non-pristine fibres are extrinsic by definition. Extrinsic strengths show larger statistical variations than can be accounted for from fibre diameter variations alone. The additional variation in srength arises from the variation in the severity of the most severe flaws in different samples. Gupta has carried out a detailed analysis of the strength distributions by combining the variations in fibre diameter and in the flaw-severity statistics.

E.G. Fluoride glass fibres are often used for both passive and active applications. Current fibres are made from fluorozirconate glasses. Their intrinsic strength is less than that of silica fibres and their surface is easily damaged by liquid water. The difference between the reported values of the fibre strength is indicative of the significance of the extrinsic defects in the mode of failure. The surface of the glass preform largely determines the mechanical properties of the fibre, and many defects arise during fibre processing. The defects in this particular type of fibre are often related to its chemical instability in the presence of water. Thus, aqueous solutions corrode fibre surface and play a detrimental role in the fibre's mechanical performance. Thus the need for a hermetic seal.

Inert Strength

Strength measured in the absence of fatigue is called the inert strength. This should not be confused with intinsic srength. Inert refers to absence of fatigue, while intrinsic refers to absence of flaws. In this article, the inert strength is denoted by S_0.

In principle, inert strength can be measured by using testing conditions which minimize fatigue. These include dry environment or vacuum and sufficiently large strain rates so that the fatigue reaction does not have time to progress). All these approaches have been attempted with varying degrees of success. However, inert strengths are rneasured most conveniently by testing at the liquid N2 temperature (77 K) where the rate of the fatigue reaction is sufficiently small as to be considered regligible. Several experiments have demonstrated that the measured strength at room temperature under conditions of high vacuum approaches the measured strength at the liquid nitrogen temperatures. ln other words, there is no significant temperature dependence of the inert strength.

The temperarured dependence from other intrinsic properties such as E is negligible. It follows that:

$$S_o = S_{LN}$$

where S_{LN} is the strength measured at the liquid N_2 temperature.

Theoretical Strength

The strengths of pristine fibres at the liquid nitrogen temperature, S^*_{LN}, are the highest strength values measured for a given composition. One might expect S^*_{LN}, in the absence of flaws, to be equal to the theoretical strength of a glass:

$$S_{th} = S^*_{LN}$$

Theoretical approximations of S_{th} are not yet available for varied compositions, and are not reliable even for simple one-component glass compositions. For example, estimates of the theoretical strength of silica as a perfect elastic crystalline solid differ by as much as 100 per cent. A number of different models relate the theoretical strength to a product of Young's modulus and surface tension? However, it is not clear yet whether or not the intrinsic strength is directly related to *E*. This may be due to the fact that *E* is determined solely by the harmonic part of the pairwise interaction potential.

In actuality, the stress required to disrupt a chemical bond is determined by the inflection point (i.e., the anharmonic part) of the pairwise interaction. Similarly, the surface tension is determined by the depth of the potential well, but contains little information about the inflection point. Thus, a product of *E* and ? will not contain the necessary information regarding the inflection point of the interaction potential. The product may therefore not be directly related to the intrinsic strength.

Molecular dynamics (MD) simulations have revealed some information on the mechanisms involved in the failure modes of silica glass. E.G. Soules has shown that the random amorphous network of SiO_4 tetrahedra (with roughly every other edge shared) weakens glassy SiO_2 glass relative to the cristobalite crystalline structure (with precisely every other edge shared) by a factor of roughly 3. In addition, Simmons has shown that structural relaxation and surface reconstruction both play important roles in the vicinity of the crack tip. However, MD simulations do not necessarily provide an accurate estimate of intrinsic strength. Again, this may be largely due to the inherent uncertainty in the anharmonic portion of the interaction potentials.

Accurate calculations of theoretical strength requires precise knowledge of the long-range behaviour of the interatomic interaction potentials, and thus the non-linear aspects of the interatomic forces. In addition, one needs some knowledge of the covalent bonds which are necessarily multi-body interactions, as well as knowledge of the intermediate range structure of the amorphous glassy network. Finally, one also needs some knowledge of the effect of topological disorder on the stress concentration, and the use of finite temperature to allow for structural changes and plastic deformation.

Index

A

Aluminium Glass Mirror, 124

Amorphous solid, 174-177

Antique glass, 7-10

Applied Ceramic Labelling, 62

Archimedes Death Ray, 130

Aristotle, 90

Aryabhatiya, 85

Astronomiae Pars Optica (The Optical Part of Astronomy), 93

B

Biblical Book of Exodus, 205

Blaschka Glass Flowers, 17

Bobby Bowden Field at Doak Campbell Stadium, 110

British Museum, 105

C

Composite material, 205-216

- autoclave moulding, 208-209
- categories of fibre-reinforced composite materials, 212
- examples, 213-215
- failure, 212-213
- history, 205-207
- moulding methods, 207-208
- pressure bag moulding, 208
- products, 215-216
- properties, 210-211
- resin transfer moulding, 209
- resins, 211-212
- tooling, 210
- vacuum bag moulding, 208

Controlled Pore Glass (CPG), 46

Corning Glass Works, 199

Corning Museum of Glass, 17

D

Decorative Glass Mirror, 124

Dharmakirti, 85

Dissolution of the Monasteries, 107

DLP, 128

F

Father of the Studio Glass Movement, 142

Fibreglass, 198-204

- chemistry, 199-201
- glass-reinforced plastic, 203-204
- properties, 201
- role of recycling in fibreglass manufacturing, 204
- safety, 201-202

G

Glass Art Society, 141

Glass beadmaking, 152-156
- cold-cut vessels, 164-167
- dichroic glass beads, 155
- drawn glass beads, 153
- furnace glass, 155
- lead crystal, 155
- molded beads, 154-155
- other methods for making glass beads, 156
- wound glass beads, 152

Glass colouring, 80-82

Glass in Islamic culture, 111-119
- art, 131-132
- Australia, 141
- Belgium, 141-142
- China, 140
- creating art made from glass, 142-143
- effects, 124-125
- entertainment, 131
- face-to-face mirrors, 130
- instruments, 128-130
- Italy, 138
- Japan, 140-141
- late Islamic glass, 116-118
- leisure, 131
- literature, 132-133
- Mexico, 141
- middle Islamic glass, 114-116
- mirrors and superstition, 133-135
- Netherlands, 141
- roles of Islamic glass, 118
- safety and easier viewing, 125-127
- seasonal lighting, 130
- study of Islamic glass, 118-119
- technological change, 112-114
- technology, 127-128
- United Kingdom, 139-140

Glass production, 59-74
- annealing, 61
- borosilicate glass, 69-70
- borosilicate nanoparticles, 74
- coatings, 62-63ancillary processes, 63
- cold end, 62
- composition and physical characteristics, 70-73
- float glass, 66-68
- forming process, 59-60
- furnace, 59
- glass container factories, 59
- global environmental impact, 66
- in lampworking, 74
- inspection equipment, 61-62
- internal treatment, 60-61
- lifecycle impact, 64-65
- local environment impacts, 65-66
- manufacture, 68-69
- manufacturing process, 70
- marketing, 63-64
- packaging, 62
- secondary processing, 62

Glass transition, 33-44
- amorphous metals, 39-41
- biomaterials, 41-42
- chalcogenides, 37-39
- colloidal glasses, 43-44
- glass-ceramics, 42-43

phosphates, 37

Glassblowing, 144-151

free-blowing, 144-145

history, 148-151

modern context, 145-148

recent developments, 151

Glass-reinforced plastic, 168-173

applications, 170-171

chopped strand mat, 173

fiberglass spray lay-up operation, 172-173

house building, 171-172

sizing, 169-170

storage tanks, 171

Goblet of the Eight Princes, 116

Guild of Glass Engravers, 140

H

Han Dynasty of China, 158

Harvard Museum of Natural History, 17

Hero of Alexandria, 85

History of optics, 83-99

beginnings of diffractive optics, 95

- - geometrical optics, 86-87

- - physical optics, 87-90

- - physiological optics, 90-91

early history of optics, 83-86

lenses and lens making, 96-97

optics in mediaeval Europe, 91-93

quantum optics, 97-99

renaissance and early modern optics, 93-95

I

International Agency for Research on Cancer, 202

Introduction, 1-17

behaviour of antique glass, 7-10

contemporary glass production, 3-4

glass ingredients, 2-3

glass vs. a supercooled liquid, 6-7

India, 14-15

Murano glassmaking, 15-17

museums, 17

optical waveguides, 10-14

physics of glass, 5-6

silica-free glasses, 4-5

Islam, 114

Islamic culture, 111-119

K

Kitab al-Durra al-Maknuna, 106

Kitab al-Manazir (The Optics), 88

L

LCD, 128

Lens, 178-182

construction of simple lenses, 180-182

Lycurgus Cup, 105

M

Metropolitan Museum of Art, 17, 205

Mirror, 120-135

manufacturing, 122-124

Moorish Spain, 121

Moulding methods, 207-208

MROS (Multiple Reflective Optic System), 125
Murano glassmaking, 15-17

N

Narcissus of Greek Mythology, 132
National Glass Centre, 139
National Liberty Museum, 138
Niijima International Glass Art Festival, 140
NIST, 39
North American Insulation Manufacturers Association (NAIMA), 202
Northlands Glass School, 140

O

Optical lens design, 75-79
  design requirements, 75-76
  lens optimization, 78-79
  process, 76-77
Optical Revolution, 87
Owens-Corning Fibreglass Corporation, 199
Owens-Illinois Glass Company, 199
Oxidizing Yellow Antimony, 167

P

Physics of glass, 18-32
  dislocations and melting, 22-24
  domains and defects, 19-22
  elastic waves, 27-29
  electronic structure, 31-32
  heat transport, 29-31
  viscoelasticity, 24-25
  vitrification, 25-27
Pittsburgh Glass Centre, 138
Porous glass, 45-49
  applications, 48-49
  definition, 46-48

R

Rhode Island School of Design in 1969, 137
River Belus, 13
Roman glass, 157-167
  glass working, 162-164
Ruby Gold, 82

S

Safety Glass Mirror, 124
Scottish Glass Society, 139
Second World War, 170
Selenium Ruby, 82
Seljuq Turks, 114
Shatapatha Brahmana, 14
Silkscreen Printed Glass Mirror, 124
Society for Cryobiology, 42
Sol-gel, 50-58
  applications, 56-58
  particles and polymers, 53-55
  polymerization, 55-56
  uniformity, 52-53
Space Shuttle Challenger, 41
Stained glass, 100-110
  creating stained glass windows, 103-105
  glass production, 101-103
  origins, 105-107
  renaissance and reformation, 107
  revival in Britain, 107-108
  - - Europe, 108-109
  - - France, 108

twentieth century, 109-110

Strength of glass, 217-226

extrinsic strength, 224

Griffith defects, 220-221

inert strength, 224-225

intrinsic strength, 222

pristine fibres, 223-224

strength types, 218-220

theoretical strength, 225-226

weibull statistics, 221-222

Studio glass, 136-143

Supercooled liquid, 6-7

Swiss Federal Institute of Technology at Lausanne, 74

T

Texas Instruments, 127

Toledo Museum of Art in 1962, 142, 145

Transparency and translucency, 183-197

applications, 196-197

light scattering in ceramics, 195-196

light scattering, 186-193

multi-phonon absorption, 193-195

U

UK Pilkington Brothers, 68

United States, 133

US Department of Health and Human Services, 202

Uzbekistan, 115

V

Vacuum bag moulding, 208

Vaisheshika, 84

Vidimus, 103

Vinaya Pitaka, 14

Vishnu Purana, 84

W

White Antimony, 167

World War II, 109

Wound glass beads, 152